Henry Irving

The Drama

Henry Irving

The Drama

ISBN/EAN: 9783337344634

Printed in Europe, USA, Canada, Australia, Japan

Cover: Foto ©Thomas Meinert / pixelio.de

More available books at **www.hansebooks.com**

THE DRAMA

Addresses by

HENRY IRVING

I. The Stage as it is
II. The Art of Acting
III. Four Great Actors
IV. The Art of Acting

WITH A FRONTISPIECE BY WHISTLER

NEW YORK
TAIT, SONS & COMPANY
Union Square

Copyright, 1892, by
UNITED STATES BOOK COMPANY

[*All rights reserved*]

CONTENTS

	PAGE
The Stage as it is	9
The Art of Acting	49
Four Great Actors	107
The Art of Acting	173

LECTURE

SESSIONAL OPENING

PHILOSOPHICAL INSTITUTION

EDINBURGH

8 NOVEMBER

1881

THE STAGE AS IT IS.

LADIES AND GENTLEMEN,

YOU will not be surprised that, on this interesting occasion, I have selected as the subject of the few remarks I propose to offer you, "The Stage as it is." The stage—because to my profession I owe it that I am here, and every dictate of taste and of fidelity impels me to honor it; the stage as it is—because it is very cheap and empty honor that is paid to the drama in the abstract, and withheld from the theatre as a working institution in our midst. Fortunately there is less of this than there used to be. It arose partly from intellectual superciliousness, partly

THE STAGE AS IT IS

from timidity as to moral contamination. To boast of being able to appreciate Shakespeare more in reading him than in seeing him acted used to be a common method of affecting special intellectuality. I hope this delusion—a gross and pitiful one as to most of us—has almost absolutely died out. It certainly conferred a very cheap badge of superiority on those who entertained it. It seemed to each of them an inexpensive opportunity of worshipping himself on a pedestal. But what did it amount to? It was little more than a conceited and feather-headed assumption that an unprepared reader, whose mind is usually full of far other things, will see on the instant all that has been developed in hundreds of years by the members of a studious and enthusiastic profession. My own conviction is, that there are few characters or passages of our great dramatists which will not repay original study. But at least

THE STAGE AS IT IS

we must recognize the vast advantages with which a practised actor, impregnated by the associations of his life, and by study—with all the practical and critical skill of his profession up to the date at which he appears, whether he adopts or rejects tradition—addresses himself to the interpretation of any great character, even if he have no originality whatever. There is something still more than this, however, in acting. Every one who has the smallest histrionic gift has a natural dramatic fertility; so that as soon as he knows the author's text, and obtains self-possession, and feels at home in a part without being too familiar with it, the mere automatic action of rehearsing and playing it at once begins to place the author in new lights, and to give the personage being played an individuality partly independent of, and yet consistent with, and rendering more powerfully visible, the dramatist's conception. It is

THE STAGE AS IT IS

the vast power a good actor has in this way which has led the French to speak of creating a part when they mean its being first played; and French authors are so conscious of the extent and value of this co-operation of actors with them, that they have never objected to the phrase, but, on the contrary, are uniformly lavish in their homage to the artists who have created on the boards the parts which they themselves have created on paper.

I must add, as an additional reason for valuing the theatre, that while there is only one Shakespeare, and while there are comparatively few dramatists who are sufficiently classic to be read with close attention, there is a great deal of average dramatic work excellently suited for representation. From this the public derive pleasure. From this they receive—as from fiction in literature—a great deal of instruction and mental stimulus.

THE STAGE AS IT IS

Some may be worldly, some social, some cynical, some merely humorous and witty, but a great deal of it, though its literary merit is secondary, is well qualified to bring out all that is most fruitful of good in common sympathies. Now, it is plain that if, because Shakespeare is good reading, people were to give the cold shoulder to the theatre, the world would lose all the vast advantage which comes to it through the dramatic faculty in forms not rising to essentially literary excellence. As respects the other feeling which used to stand more than it does now in the way of the theatre—the fear of moral contamination—it is due to the theatre of our day, on the one hand, and to the prejudices of our grandfathers on the other, to confess that the theatre of fifty years ago or less did need reforming in the audience part of the house. All who have read the old controversy as to the morality of going to the theatre are

THE STAGE AS IT IS

familiar with the objection to which I refer. But the theatre of fifty years ago or less was reformed. If there are any, therefore, as I fear there are a few, who still talk on this point in the old vein, let them rub their eyes a bit, and do us the justice to consider not what used to be, but what is. But may there be moral contamination from what is performed on the stage? Well, there may be. But so there is from books. So there may be at lawn tennis clubs. So there may be at dances. So there may be in connection with everything in civilized life and society. But do we therefore bury ourselves? The anchorites secluded themselves in hermitages. The Puritans isolated themselves in consistent abstinence from everything that anybody else did. And there are people now who think that they can keep their children, and that those children will keep themselves in after life, in cotton wool, so as to avoid

THE STAGE AS IT IS

all temptation of body and mind, and be saved nine-tenths of the responsibility of self-control. All this is mere phantasy. You must be in the world, though you need not be of it; and the best way to make the world a better community to be in, and not so bad a place to be of, is not to shun, but to bring public opinion to bear upon its pursuits and its relaxations. Depend upon two things—that the theatre, as a whole, is never below the average moral sense of the time; and that the inevitable demand for an admixture, at least, of wholesome sentiment in every sort of dramatic production brings the ruling tone of the theatre, whatever drawback may exist, up to the highest level at which the general morality of the time can truly be registered. We may be encouraged by the reflection that this is truer than ever it was before, owing to the greater spread of education, the increased community of taste between classes, and the almost absolute divorce of the stage from mere wealth and aristocracy. Wealth and aristocracy come around the stage in abundance, and are welcome, as in the time of Elizabeth; but the stage is no longer a mere appendage of court-life, no longer a mere mirror of patrician vice hanging at the girdle of fashionable profligacy as it was in the days of Congreve and Wycherley. It is now the property of the educated people. It has to satisfy them or pine in neglect. And the better their demands the better will be the supply with which the drama will respond. This being not only so, but seen to be so, the stage is no longer proscribed. It is no longer under a ban. Its members are no longer pariahs in society. They live and bear their social part like others—as decorously observant of all that makes the sweet sanctities of life—as gracefully cognizant of its amenities—as readily recognized and

THE STAGE AS IT IS

welcomed as the members of any other profession. Am I not here your grateful guest, opening the session of this philosophical and historic institution? I who am simply an actor, an interpreter, with such gifts as I have, and such thought as I can bestow, of stage plays. And am I not received here with perfect cordiality on an equality, not hungrily bowing and smirking for patronage, but interchanging ideas which I am glad to express, and which you listen to as thoughtfully and as kindly as you would to those of any other student, any other man who had won his way into such prominence as to come under the ken of a distinguished institution such as that which I have the honor to address? I do not mince the matter as to my personal position here, because I feel it is a representative one, and marks an epoch in the estimation in which the art I love is held by the British

THE STAGE AS IT IS

world. You have had many distinguished men here, and their themes have often been noble, but with which of those themes has not my art immemorial and perpetual associations? Is it not for ever identified with the noblest instincts and occupations of the human mind? If I think of poetry, must I not remember how to the measure of its lofty music the theatre has in almost all ages set the grandest of dramatic conceptions? If I think of literature, must I not recall that of all the amusements by which men in various states of society have solaced their leisure and refreshed their energies, the acting of plays is the one that has never yet, even for a day, been divorced from literary taste and skill? If I meditate on patriotism, can I but reflect how grandly the boards have been trod by personifications of heroic love of country? There is no subject of human thought that by common con-

THE STAGE AS IT IS

sent is deemed ennobling that has not ere now, and from period to period, been illustrated in the bright vesture, and received expression from the glowing language of theatrical representation. And surely it is fit that, remembering what the stage has been and must be, I should acknowledge eagerly and gladly that, with few exceptions, the public no longer debar themselves from the profitable pleasures of the theatre, and no longer brand with any social stigma the professors of the histrionic art. Talking to an eminent bishop one day, I said to him, "Now, my Lord, why is it, with your love and knowledge of the drama, with your deep interest in the stage and all its belongings, and your wide sympathy with all that ennobles and refines our natures—why is it that you never go to the theatre?" "Well," said he, "I'll tell you. I'm afraid of the *Rock* and the *Record*." I hope soon we shall relieve even the most

THE STAGE AS IT IS

timid bishop—and my right reverend friend is not the most timid—of all fears and tremors whatever that can prevent even ministers of religion from recognizing the wisdom of the change of view which has come over even the most fastidious public opinion on this question. Remember, if you please, that the hostile public opinion which has lately begun so decisively to disappear, has been of comparatively modern growth, or at least revival. The pious and learned of other times gave their countenance and approbation to the stage of their days, as the pious and learned of our time give their countenance and approbation to certain performances in this day. Welcome be the return of good sense, good taste, and charity, or rather justice. No apology for the stage. None is needed. It has but to be named to be honored. Too long the world talked with bated breath and whispering hum-

THE STAGE AS IT IS

bleness of "the poor player." There are now few poor players. Whatever variety of fortune and merit there may be among them, they have the same degrees of prosperity and respect as come to members of other avocations. There never was so large a number of theatres or of actors. And their type is vastly improved by public recognition. The old days when good-for-nothings passed into the profession are at an end; and the old Bohemian habits, so far as they were evil and disreputable, have also disappeared. The ranks of the art are being continually recruited by deeply interested and earnest young men of good education and belongings. Nor let us, while dissipating the remaining prejudices of outsiders, give quarter to those which linger among players themselves. There are some who acknowledge the value of improved status to themselves and their art, but who lament that there are now

THE STAGE AS IT IS

no schools for actors. This is a very idle lamentation. Every actor in full employment gets plenty of schooling, for the best schooling is practice, and there is no school so good as a well-conducted playhouse. The truth is, that the cardinal secret of success in acting are found within, while practice is the surest way of fertilizing these germs. To efficiency in the art of acting there should come a congregation of fine qualities. There should be considerable, though not necessarily systematic, culture. There should be delicate instincts of taste cultivated, consciously, or unconsciously, to a degree of extreme and subtle nicety. There should be a power, at once refined and strong, of both perceiving and expressing to others the significance of language, so that neither shades nor masses of meaning, so to speak, may be either lost or exaggerated. Above all, there should be a sincere and abounding sympathy with all that is good and great and inspiring. That sympathy, most certainly, must be under the control and manipulation of art, but it must be none the lest real and generous, and the artist who is a mere artist will stop short of the highest moral effects of his craft, Little of this can be got in a mere training school, but all of it will come forth more or less fully armed from the actor's brain in the process of learning his art by practice. For the way to learn to do a thing is to do it ; and in learning to act by acting, though there is plenty of incidental hard drill and hard work, there is nothing commonplace or unfruitful.

What is true of the art is true also of the social life of the artist. No sensational change has been found necessary to alter his status though great changes have come. The stage has literally lived down the rebuke and reproach under which it formerly cowered, while its professors have been simultaneously living down the prejudices which excluded them from society. The stage is now seen to be an elevating instead of a lowering influence on national morality, and actors and actresses receive in society, as do the members of other professions, exactly the treatment which is earned by their personal conduct. And so I would say of what we sometimes hear so much about—dramatic reform. It is not needed ; or, if it is, all the reform that is wanted will be best effected by the operation of public opinion upon the administration of a good theatre. That is the true reforming agency, with this great advantage, that reforms which come by public opinion are sure, while those which come without public opinion cannot be relied upon. The dramatic reformers are very well-meaning people. They show great enthusiasm. They are new converts to

THE STAGE AS IT IS

the theatre, most of them, and they have the zeal of converts. But it is scarcely according to knowledge. These ladies and gentlemen have scarcely studied the conditions of theatrical enterprise, which must be carried on as a business or it will fail as an art. It is an unwelcome, if not an unwarrantable intrusion to come among our people with elaborate advice, and endeavor to make them live after different fashions from those which are suitable to them, and it will be quite hopeless to attempt to induce the general body of a purely artistic class to make louder and more fussy professions of virtue and religion than other people. In fact, it is a downright insult to the dramatic profession to exact or to expect any such thing. Equally objectionable, and equally impracticable, are the attempts of Quixotic "dramatic reformers" to exercise a sort of goody-goody censorship over the selection

THE STAGE AS IT IS

and the text of the plays to be acted. The stage has been serving the world for hundreds, yes, and thousands of years, during which it has contributed in pure dramaturgy to the literature of the world its very greatest master-pieces in nearly all languages, meanwhile affording to the million an infinity of pleasure, all more or less innocent. Where less innocent, rather than more, the cause has lain, not in the stage, but in the state of society of which it was the mirror. For though the stage is not always occupied with its own period, the new plays produced always reflect in many particulars the spirit of the age in which they are played. There is a story of a traveller who put up for the night at a certain inn, on the door of which was the inscription —"Good entertainment for man and beast." His horse was taken to the stable and well cared for, and he sat down to dine. When the covers were removed he

THE STAGE AS IT IS

remarked, on seeing his own sorry fare, "Yes, this is very well; but where's the entertainment for the man?" If everything were banished from the stage except that which suits a certain taste, what dismal places our theatres would be! However fond the play-goer may be of tragedy, if you offer him nothing but horrors, he may well ask—"Where's the entertainment for the man who wants an evening's amusement?" The humor of a farce may not seem over-refined to a particular class of intelligence; but there are thousands of people who take an honest pleasure in it. And who, after seeing my old friend J. L. Toole in some of his famous parts, and having laughed till their sides ached, have not left the theatre more buoyant and light-hearted than they came? Well, if the stage has been thus useful and successful all these centuries, and still is productive; if the noble fascination of the theatre

THE STAGE AS IT IS

draws to it, as we know that it does, an immortal poet such as our Tennyson, whom, I can testify from my own experience, nothing delights more than the success of one of the plays which, in the mellow autumn of his genius, he has contributed to the acting theatre; if a great artist like Tadema is proud to design scenes for stage plays; if in all departments of stage production we see great talent, and in nearly every instance great good taste and sincere sympathy with the best popular ideals of goodness; then, I say, the stage is entitled to be let alone—that is, it is entitled to make its own bargain with the public without the censorious intervention of well-intentioned busybodies. These do not know what to ban or to bless. If they had their way, as of course they cannot, they would license, with many flourishes and much self-laudation, a number of pieces which would be hopelessly condemned on the first hearing, and

THE STAGE AS IT IS

they would lay an embargo for very insufficient reasons on many plays well entitled to success. It is not in this direction that we must look for any improvement that is needed in the purveying of material for the stage. Believe me, the right direction is public criticism and public discrimination. I say so because, beyond question, the public will have what they want. So far, that managers in their discretion, or at their pleasure, can force on the public either very good or very bad dramatic material is an utter delusion. They have no such power. If they had the will they could only force any particular sort of entertainment just as long as they had capital to expend without any return. But they really have not the will. They follow the public taste with the greatest keenness. If the people want Shakespeare—as I am happy to say they do, at least at one theatre in London, and at all the great theatres out of London,

THE STAGE AS IT IS

to an extent unprecedented in the history of the stage—then they get Shakespeare. If they want our modern dramatists—Albery, Boucicault, Byron, Burnand, Gilbert, or Wills—these they have. If they want Robertson, Robertson is there for them. If they desire opera-bouffe, depend upon it they will have it, and have it they do. What then do I infer? Simply this: that those who prefer the higher drama—in the representation of which my heart's best interests are centred—instead of querulously animadverting on managers who give them something different, should, as Lord Beaconsfield said, "make themselves into a majority." If they do so, the higher drama will be produced. But if we really understand the value of the drama, we shall not be too rigid in our exactions. The drama is the art of human nature in picturesque or characteristic action. Let us be liberal in our enjoyment of it.

THE STAGE AS IT IS

Tragedy, comedy, historical-pastoral, pastoral-comical—remember the large-minded list of the greatest-minded poet—all are good, if wholesome—and will be wholesome if the public continue to take the healthy interest in theatres which they are now taking. The worst times for the stage have been those when playgoing was left pretty much to a loose society, such as is sketched in the Restoration dramatists. If the good people continue to come to the theatre in increasing crowds, the stage, without losing any of its brightness, will soon be good enough, if it is not as yet, to satisfy the best of them. This is what I believe all sensible people in these times see. And if, on the one hand, you are ready to laugh at the old prejudices which have been so happily dissipated; on the other hand, how earnestly must you welcome the great aid to taste and thought and culture which comes to you thus in the guise of amusement. Let me put this to you rather seriously ; let me insist on the intellectual and moral use, alike to the most and least cultivated of us, of this art " most beautiful, most difficult, most rare," which I stand here to-day, not to apologize for, but to establish in the high place to which it is entitled among the arts and among the ameliorating influences of life. Grant that any of us understand a dramatist better for seeing him acted, and it follows, first, that all of us will be most indebted to the stage at the point where the higher and more ethereal faculties are liable in reading to failure and exhaustion, that is, stage-playing will be of most use to us where the mind requires help and inspiration to grasp and revel in lofty moral or imaginative conceptions, or where it needs aid and sharpening to appreciate and follow the niceties of repartee, or the delicacies of comic fancy. Secondly, it follows

THE STAGE AS IT IS

that if this is so with the intellectual few, it must be infinitely more so with the unimaginative many of all ranks. They are not inaccessible to passion and poetry and refinement, but their minds do not go forth, as it were, to seek these joys; and even if they read works of poetic and dramatic fancy, which they rarely do, they would miss them on the printed page. To them, therefore, with the exception of a few startling incidents of real life, the theatre is the only channel through which are ever brought the great sympathies of the world of thought beyond their immediate ken. And thirdly, it follows from all this that the stage is, intellectually and morally, to all who have recourse to it, the source of some of the finest and best influences of which they are respectively susceptible. To the thoughtful and reading man it brings the life, the fire, the color, the vivid instinct, which are beyond the reach of

THE STAGE AS IT IS

study. To the common indifferent man, immersed, as a rule, in the business and socialities of daily life, it brings visions of glory and adventure, of emotion and of broad human interest. It gives glimpses of the heights and depths of character and experience, setting him thinking and wondering even in the midst of amusement. To the most torpid and unobservant it exhibits the humorous in life and the sparkle and finesse of language, which in dull ordinary existence is stupidly shut out of knowledge or omitted from particular notice. To all it uncurtains a world, not that in which they live and yet not other than it—a world in which interest is heightened whilst the conditions of truth are observed, in which the capabilities of men and women are seen developed without losing their consistency to nature, and developed with a curious and wholesome fidelity to simple and universal instincts of clear right and wrong.

THE STAGE AS IT IS

Be it observed—and I put it most uncompromisingly—I am not speaking or thinking of any unrealizable ideal, not of any lofty imagination of what might be, but of what is, wherever there are pit and gallery and foot-lights. More or less, and taking one evening with another, you may find support for an enthusiastic theory of stage morality and the high tone of audiences in most theatres in the country; and if you fancy that it is least so in the theatres frequented by the poor you make a great mistake, for in none is the appreciation of good moral fare more marked than in these.

In reference to the poorer classes, we all lament the wide prevalence of intemperate drinking. Well, is it not an obvious reflection that the worst performance seen on any of our stages cannot be so bad as drinking for a corresponding time in a gin-palace? I have pointed this contrast before, and I point it again.

THE STAGE AS IT IS

The drinking we deplore takes place in company—bad company; it is enlivened by talk—bad talk. It is relished by obscenity. Where drink and low people come together these things must be. The worst that can come of stage pandering to the corrupt tastes of its basest patrons cannot be anything like this, and, as a rule, the stage holds out long against the invitation to pander; and such invitations, from the publicity and decorum that attend the whole matter, are neither frequent nor eager. A sort of decency sets in upon the coarsest person in entering even the roughest theatre. I have sometimes thought that, considering the liability to descend and the facility of descent, a special Providence watches over the morals and tone of our English stage. I do not desire to overcharge the eulogy. There never was a time when the stage had not conspicuous faults. There never was a time

THE STAGE AS IT IS

when these were not freely admitted by those most concerned for the maintenance of the stage at its best. In Shakespeare, whenever the subject of the theatre is approached, we perceive signs that that great spirit, though it had a practical and business-like vein, and essayed no impossible enterprises, groaned under the necessities, or the demands of a public which desired frivolities and deformities which jarred upon the poet-manager's feelings. As we descend the course of time we find that each generation looked back to a supposed previous period when taste ranged higher, and when the inferior and offensive peculiarities of the existing stage were unknown. Yet from most of these generations we inherit works as well as traditions and biographical recollections which the world will never let die. The truth is that the immortal part of the stage is its nobler part. Ignoble accidents and interludes come and go, but this lasts on forever. It lives, like the human soul, in the body of humanity—associated with much that is inferior, and hampered by many hindrances—but it never sinks into nothingness, and never fails to find new and noble work in creations of permanent and memorable excellence. Heaven forbid that I should seem to cover, even with a counterpane of courtesy, exhibitions of deliberate immorality. Happily this sort of thing is not common, and although it has hardly been practised by any one who, without a strain of meaning can be associated with the profession of acting, yet public censure, not active enough to repress the evil, is ever ready to pass a sweeping condemnation on the stage which harbors it. Our cause is a good one. We go forth, armed with the luminous panoply which genius has forged for us, to do battle with dulness, with coarseness, with apathy, with every

THE STAGE AS IT IS

form of vice and evil. In every human heart there gleams a bright reflection of this shining armor. The stage has no lights or shadows that are not lights of life and shadows of the heart. To each human consciousness it appeals in alternating mirth and sadness, and will not be denied. Err it must, for it is human; but, being human, it must endure. The love of acting is inherent in our nature. Watch your children play, and you will see that almost their first conscious effort is to act and to imitate. It is an instinct, and you can no more repress it than you can extinguish thought. When this instinct of all is developed by cultivation in the few, it becomes a wonderful art, priceless to civilization in the solace it yields, the thought it generates, the refinement it inspires. Some of its latest achievements are not unworthy of their grandest predecessors. Some of its youngest devotees are at least as proud

THE STAGE AS IT IS

of its glories and as anxious to preserve them as any who have gone before. Theirs is a glorious heritage! You honor it. They have a noble but a difficult, and sometimes a disheartening, task. You encourage it. And no word of kindly interest or criticism dropped in the public ear from friendly lips goes unregarded or is unfertile of good. The universal study of Shakespeare in our public schools is a splendid sign of the departure of prejudice, and all criticism is welcome; but it is acting chiefly that can open to others, with any spark of Shakespeare's mind, the means of illuminating the world. Only the theatre can realize to us in a life-like way what Shakespeare was to his own time. And it is, indeed, a noble destiny for the theatre to vindicate in these later days the greatness which sometimes it has seemed to vulgarize. It has been too much the custom to talk of Shakespeare as nature's child—as the lad who held horses for people who came to the play—as a sort of chance phenomenon who wrote these plays by accident and unrecognized. How supremely ridiculous! How utterly irreconcilable with the grand dimensions of the man! How absurdly dishonoring to the great age of which he was, and was known to be, the glory! The noblest literary man of all time—the finest and yet most prolific writer—the greatest student of man, and the greatest master of man's highest gift of language —surely it is treason to humanity to speak of such an one as in any sense a commonplace being! Imagine him rather, as he must have been, the most notable courtier of the Court—the most perfect gentleman who stood in the Elizabethan throng—the man in whose presence divines would falter and hesitate lest their knowledge of the Book should seem poor by the side of his, and at

THE STAGE AS IT IS

whom even queenly royalty would look askance, with an oppressive sense that here was one to whose omnipotent and true imagination the hearts of kings and queens and peoples had always been an open page! The thought of such a man is an incomparable inheritance for any nation, and such a man was the actor—Shakespeare. Such is our birthright and yours. Such the succession in which it is ours to labor and yours to enjoy. For Shakespeare belongs to the stage for ever, and his glories must always inalienably belong to it. If you uphold the theatre honestly, liberally, frankly, and with wise discrimination, the stage will uphold in future, as it has in the past, the literature, the manners, the morals, the fame, and the genius of our country. There must have been something wrong, as there was something poignant and lacerating, in prejudices which so long partly divorced the con-

THE STAGE AS IT IS

science of Britain from its noblest pride, and stamped with reproach, or at least depreciation, some of the brightest and world-famous incidents of her history. For myself, it kindles my heart with proud delight to think that I have stood to-day before this audience—known for its discrimination throughout all English-speaking lands—a welcome and honored guests, because I stand here for justice to the art to which I am devoted—because I stand here in thankfulness for the justice which has begun to be so abundantly rendered to it. If it is metaphorically the destiny of humanity, it is literally the experience of an actor, that one man in his time plays many parts. A player of any standing must at various times have sounded the gamut of human sensibility from the lowest note to the top of its compass. He must have banqueted often on curious food for thought as he meditated on the subtle relations

THE STAGE AS IT IS

created between himself and his audiences, as they have watched in his impersonations the shifting tariff—the ever gliding, delicately graduated sliding-scale of dramatic right and wrong. He may have gloated, if he be a cynic, over the depths of ghastly horror, or the vagaries of moral puddle through which it may have been his duty to plash. But if he be an honest man, he will acknowledge that scarcely ever has either dramatist or management wilfully biassed the effect of stage representation in favor of evil, and of his audiences he will boast that never has their mind been doubtful—never has their true perception of the generous and just been known to fail, or even to be slow. How noble the privilege to work upon these finer—these finest—feelings of universal humanity! How engrossing the fascination of those thousands of steady eyes, and sound sympathies, and beating hearts which an

THE STAGE AS IT IS

actor confronts, with the confidence of friendship and co-operation, as he steps upon the stage to work out in action his long-pent comprehension of a noble master-piece! How rapturous the satisfaction of abandoning himself, in such a presence and with such sympathizers, to his author's grandest flights of thought and noblest bursts of emotional inspiration! And how perpetually sustaining the knowledge that whatever may be the vicissitudes and even the degradations of the stage, it must and will depend for its constant hold on the affection and attention of mankind upon its loftier work; upon its more penetrating passion; upon its themes which most deeply search out the strong affections and high hopes of men and women; upon its fit and kindling illustration of great and vivid lives which either have been lived in noble fact or have deserved to endure immortally in the popular

THE STAGE AS IT IS

belief and admiration which they have secured.

> " For our eyes to see!
> Sons of wisdom, song, and power,
> Giving earth her richest dower,
> And making nations free—
> A glorious company!
>
> " Call them from the dead
> For our eyes to see!
> Forms of beauty, love, and grace,
> ' Sunshine in the shady place,'
> That made it life to be—
> A blessed company! "

ADDRESS

TO THE STUDENTS

OF THE UNIVERSITY OF

HARVARD

30TH MARCH

1885

THE ART OF ACTING

I

THE OCCASION.

AM deeply sensible of the compliment that has been paid, not so much to me personally as to the calling I represent, by the invitation to deliver an address to the students of this University. As an actor, and especially as an English actor, it is a great pleasure to speak for my art in one of the chief centres of American culture; for in inviting me here to-day you intended, I believe, to recognize the drama as an educational influence, to show a

genuine interest in the stage as a factor in life which must be accepted and not ignored by intelligent people. I have thought that the best use I can make of the privilege you have conferred upon me is to offer you, as well as I am able, something like a practical exposition of my art; for it may chance—who knows?—that some of you may at some future time be disposed to adopt it as a vocation. Not that I wish to be regarded as a tempter who has come among you to seduce you from your present studies by artful pictures of the fascinations of the footlights. But I naturally supposed that you would like me to choose, as the theme of my address, the subject in which I am most interested, and to which my life has been devoted; and that if any students here should ever determine to become actors, they could not be much the worse for the information and counsel I could gather for them from a tolerably

THE ART OF ACTING

extensive experience. This subject will, I trust, be welcome to all of you who are interested in the stage as an institution which appeals to the sober-minded and intelligent; for I take it that you have no lingering prejudice against the theatre, or else I should not be here. Nor are you disposed, like certain good people, to object to the theatre simply as a name. These sticklers for principle would never enter a playhouse for worlds; and I have heard that in a famous city of Massachusetts, not a hundred miles from here, there are persons to whom the theatre is unknown, but who have no objection to see a play in a building which is called a museum, especially if the vestibule leading to the theatre should be decorated with sound moral principles in the shape of statues, pictures, and stuffed objects in glass cases.

When I began to think about my subject for the purpose of this address, I was

THE ART OF ACTING

rather staggered by its vastness. It is really a matter for a course of lectures; but as President Eliot has not proposed that I should occupy a chair of dramatic literature in this University, and as time and opportunity are limited, I can only undertake to put before you, in the simplest way, a few leading ideas about dramatic art which may be worthy of reflection. And in doing this I have the great satisfaction of appearing in a model theatre, before a model audience, and of being the only actor in my own play. Moreover, I am stimulated by the atmosphere of the Greek drama, for I know that on this stage you have enacted a Greek play with remarkable success. So, after all, it is not a body of mere tyros that I am addressing, but actors who have worn the sock and buskin, and declaimed the speeches which delighted audiences two thousand years ago.

Now, this address, like discourses in a

THE ART OF ACTING

more solemn place, falls naturally into divisions. I propose to speak first of the Art of Acting; secondly, of its Requirements and Practice; and lastly of its Rewards. And, at the outset, let me say that I want you to judge the stage at its best. I do not intend to suggest that only the plays of Shakespeare are tolerable in the theatre to people of taste and intelligence. The drama has many forms—tragedy, comedy, historical-pastoral, pastoral-comical—and all are good when their aim is honestly artistic.

II

THE ART OF ACTING.

Now, what is the art of acting? I speak of it in its highest sense, as the art to which Roscius, Betterton, and Garrick owed their fame. It is the art of embodying the poet's creations, of giving them flesh and blood, of making the figures which appeal to your mind's eye in the printed drama live before you on the stage. "To fathom the depths of character, to trace its latent motives, to feel its finest quiverings of emotion, to comprehend the thoughts that are hidden under words, and thus possess one's-self of the actual mind of the individual man" —such was Macready's definition of the player's art; and to this we may add the testimony of Talma. He describes tragic acting as "the union of grandeur without pomp and nature without triviality." It demands, he says, the endowment of high sensibility and intelligence.

"The actor who possesses this double gift adopts a course of study peculiar to himself. In the first place, by repeated exercises, he enters deeply into the emotions, and his speech acquires the accent proper to the situation of the personage he has to represent. This done, he goes to the theatre not only to give theatrical effect to his studies, but also to yield himself to the spontaneous flashes of his sensibility and all the emotions which it involuntarily produces in him. What does he then do? In order that his inspirations may not be lost, his memory, in the silence of repose, recalls the accent of his voice, the expression of his features, his action—in a word, the spontaneous workings of his mind, which he had suffered to have free course, and, in effect, everything which in the moments of his exaltation contributed to the effects he had produced. His intelligence then passes all these means in review, connecting them and fixing them in his memory to re-employ them at pleasure in succeeding representations. These impressions are often so evanescent that on retiring behind the scenes he must repeat to himself what he had been playing rather than what he had to play. By this kind of labor the intelligence accumulates and preserves all the creations of sensibility. It is by this means that at the end of twenty years (it requires at least this length of time) a person destined to display fine talent may at length present to the public a series of characters acted almost to perfection."

You will readily understand from this that to the actor the well-worn maxim that art is long and life is short has a constant significance. The older we grow the more acutely alive we are to the

THE ART OF ACTING

difficulties of our craft. I cannot give you a better illustration of this fact than a story which is told of Macready. A friend of mine, once a dear friend of his, was with him when he played Hamlet for the last time. The curtain had fallen, and the great actor was sadly thinking that the part he loved so much would never be his again. And as he took off his velvet mantle and laid it aside, he muttered almost unconsciously the words of Horatio, "Good-night, sweet Prince;" then turning to his friend, "Ah," said he, "I am just beginning to realize the sweetness, the tenderness, the gentleness of this dear Hamlet!" Believe me, the true artist never lingers fondly upon what he has done. He is ever thinking of what remains undone: ever striving toward an ideal it may never be his fortune to attain.

We are sometimes told that to read the best dramatic poetry is more educating

THE ART OF ACTING

than to see it acted. I do not think this theory is very widely held, for it is in conflict with the dramatic instinct, which everybody possesses in a greater or less degree. You never met a playwright who could conceive himself willing—even if endowed with the highest literary gifts—to prefer a reading to a playgoing public. He thinks his work deserving of all the rewards of print and publisher, but he will be much more elated if it should appeal to the world in the theatre as a skilful representation of human passions. In one of her letters George Eliot says: "In opposition to most people who love to *read* Shakespeare, I like to see his plays acted better than any others; his great tragedies thrill me, let them be acted how they may." All this is so simple and intelligible, that it seems scarcely worth while to argue that in proportion to the readiness with which the reader of Shakespeare imagines the attributes of

THE ART OF ACTING

the various characters, and is interested in their personality, he will, as a rule, be eager to see their tragedy or comedy in action. He will then find that very much which he could not imagine with any definiteness presents new images every moment—the eloquence of look and gesture, the by-play, the inexhaustible significance of the human voice. There are people who fancy they have more music in their souls than was ever translated into harmony by Beethoven or Mozart. There are others who think they could paint pictures, write poetry—in short, do anything, if they only made the effort. To them what is accomplished by the practised actor seems easy and simple. But as it needs the skill of the musician to draw the full volume of eloquence from the written score, so it needs the skill of the dramatic artist to develop the subtle harmonies of the poetic play. In fact, to *do* and not to *dream*, is the mainspring of success in life. The actor's art is to act, and the true acting of any character is one of the most difficult accomplishments. I challenge the acute student to ponder over Hamlet's renunciation of Ophelia—one of the most complex scenes in all the drama—and say that he has learned more from his meditations than he could be taught by players whose intelligence is equal to his own. To present the man thinking aloud is the most difficult achievement of our art. Here the actor who has no real grip of the character, but simply recites the speeches with a certain grace and intelligence, will be untrue. The more intent he is upon the words, and the less on the ideas that dictated them, the more likely he is to lay himself open to the charge of mechanical interpretation. It is perfectly possible to express to an audience all the involutions of thought, the speculation, doubt, waver-

THE ART OF ACTING

ing, which reveal the meditative but irresolute mind. As the varying shades of fancy pass and repass the mirror of the face, they may yield more material to the studious playgoer than he is likely to get by a diligent poring over the text. In short, as we understand the people around us much better by personal intercourse than by all the revelations of written words—for words, as Tennyson says, "half reveal and half conceal the soul within," so the drama has, on the whole, infinitely more suggestions when it is well acted than when it is interpreted by the unaided judgment of the student. It has been said that acting is an unworthy occupation because it represents feigned emotions, but this censure would apply with equal force to poet or novelist. Do not imagine that I am claiming for the actor sole and undivided authority. He should himself be a student, and it is

THE ART OF ACTING

his business to put into practice the best ideas he can gather from the general current of thought with regard to the highest dramatic literature. But it is he who gives body to those ideas—fire, force, and sensibility, without which they would remain for most people mere airy abstractions.

It is often supposed that great actors trust to the inspiration of the moment. Nothing can be more erroneous. There will, of course, be such moments, when an actor at a white heat illumines some passage with a flash of imagination (and this mental condition, by the way, is impossible to the student sitting in his arm-chair); but the great actor's surprises are generally well weighed, studied, and balanced. We know that Edmund Kean constantly practised before a mirror effects which startled his audience by their apparent spontaneity. It is the accumulation of such effects which enables

THE ART OF ACTING

an actor, after many years, to present many great characters with remarkable completeness.

I do not want to overstate the case, or to appeal to anything that is not within common experience, so I can confidently ask you whether a scene in a great play has not been at some time vividly impressed on your minds by the delivery of a single line, or even of one forcible word. Has not this made the passage far more real and human to you than all the thought you have devoted to it? An accomplished critic has said that Shakespeare himself might have been surprised had he heard the "Fool, fool, fool!" of Edmund Kean. And though all actors are not Keans, they have in varying degree this power of making a dramatic character step out of the page, and come nearer to our hearts and our understandings.

After all, the best and most convincing

THE ART OF ACTING

exposition of the whole art of acting is given by Shakespeare himself: "To hold, as 'twere, the mirror up to nature, to show virtue her own feature, scorn her own image, and the very age and body of the time his form and pressure." Thus the poet recognized the actor's art as a most potent ally in the representation of human life. He believed that to hold the mirror up to nature was one of the worthiest functions in the sphere of labor, and actors are content to point to his definition of their work as the charter of their privileges.

THE ART OF ACTING

III.

PRACTICE OF THE ART.

THE practice of the art of acting is a subject difficult to treat with the necessary brevity. Beginners are naturally anxious to know what course they should pursue. In common with other actors, I receive letters from young people many of whom are very earnest in their ambition to adopt the dramatic calling, but not sufficiently alive to the fact that success does not depend on a few lessons in declamation. When I was a boy I had a habit which I think would be useful to all young students. Before going to see a play of Shakespeare's I used to form—in a very juvenile way—a theory as to the working out of the whole drama, so as to correct my conceptions by those of the actors; and

THE ART OF ACTING

though I was, as a rule, absurdly wrong, there can be no doubt that any method of independent study is of enormous importance, not only to youngsters, but also to students of a larger growth. Without it the mind is apt to take its stamp from the first forcible impression it receives, and to fall into a servile dependence upon traditions, which, robbed of the spirit that created them, are apt to be purely mischievous. What was natural to the creator is often unnatural and lifeless in the imitator. No two people form the same conceptions of character, and therefore it is always advantageous to see an independent and courageous exposition of an original ideal. There can be no objection to the kind of training that imparts a knowledge of manners and customs, and the teaching which pertains to simple deportment on the stage is necessary and most useful ; but you cannot possibly be

THE ART OF ACTING

taught any tradition of character, for that has no permanence. Nothing is more fleeting than any traditional method ot impersonation. You may learn where a particular personage used to stand on the stage, or down which trap the ghost of Hamlet's father vanished; but the soul of interpretation is lost, and it is this soul which the actor has to re-create for himself. It is not mere attitude or tone that has to be studied; you must be moved by the impulse of being; you must impersonate and not recite.

There has always been a controversy as to the province of naturalism in dramatic art. In England it has been too much the custom, I believe, while demanding naturalism in comedy, to expect a false inflation in tragedy. But there is no reason why an actor should be less natural in tragic than in lighter moods. Passions vary in expression according to moulds of character and manners, but their reality should not be lost even when they are expressed in the heroic forms of the drama. A very simple test is a reference to the records of old actors. What was it in their performances that chiefly impressed their contemporaries? Very rarely the measured recitation of this or that speech, but very often a simple exclamation that deeply moved their auditors, because it was a gleam of nature in the midst of declamation. The "Prithee, undo this button!" of Garrick, was remembered when many stately utterances were forgotten. In our day the contrast between artificial declamation and the accents of nature is less marked, because its delivery is more uniformly simple, and an actor who lapses from a natural into a false tone is sure to find that his hold upon his audience is proportionately weakened. But the revolution which Garrick accomplished may be im-

THE ART OF ACTING

agined from the story told by Boswell. Dr. Johnson was discussing plays and players with Mrs. Siddons, and he said : "Garrick, madam, was no declaimer ; there was not one of his own scene-shifters who could not have spoken 'To be or not to be' better than he did ; yet he was the only actor I ever saw whom I could call a master, both in tragedy and comedy, though I liked him best in comedy. A true conception of character and natural expression of it were his distinguished excellences."

To be natural on the stage is most difficult, and yet a grain of nature is worth a bushel of artifice. But you may say— what is nature? I quoted just now Shakespeare's definition of the actor's art. After the exhortation to hold the mirror up to nature, he adds the pregnant warning : "This overdone or come tardy off, though it make the unskilful laugh, cannot but make the judicious grieve, the censure of which one must in your allowance o'erweigh a whole theatre of others." Nature may be overdone by triviality in conditions that demand exaltation; for instance, Hamlet's first address to the Ghost lifts his disposition to an altitude far beyond the ordinary reaches of our souls, and his manner of speech should be adapted to this sentiment. But such exaltation of utterance is wholly out of place in the purely colloquial scene with the Gravedigger. When Macbeth says, "Go, bid thy mistress, when my drink is ready, she strike upon the bell," he would not use the tone of

> " Pity, like a naked new-born babe,
> Striding the blast, or Heaven's cherubim, horsed
> Upon the sightless couriers of the air,
> Shall blow the horrid deed in every eye,
> That tears shall drown the wind."

Like the practised orator, the actor rises and descends with his sentiment,

THE ART OF ACTING

and cannot always be in a fine phrenzy. This variety is especially necessary in Shakespeare, whose work is essentially different from the classic drama, because it presents every mood of mind and form of speech, commonplace or exalted, as character and situation dictate: whereas in such a play as Addison's *Cato*, everybody is consistently eloquent about everything.

There are many causes for the growth of naturalism in dramatic art, and amongst them we should remember the improvement in the mechanism of the stage. For instance, there has been a remarkable development in stage-lighting. In old pictures you will observe the actors constantly standing in a line, because the oil-lamps of those days gave such an indifferent illumination that everybody tried to get into what was called the focus—the "blaze of publicity" furnished by the "float" or foot-

THE ART OF ACTING

lights. The importance of this is illustrated by an amusing story of Edmund Kean, who one night played *Othello* with more than his usual intensity. An admirer who met him in the street next day was loud in his congratulations : "I really thought you would have choked Iago, Mr. Kean—you seemed so tremendously in earnest." "In earnest!" said the tragedian, "I should think so! Hang the fellow, he was trying to keep me out of the focus."

I do not recommend actors to allow their feelings to carry them away like this ; but it is necessary to warn you against the theory expounded with brilliant ingenuity by Diderot, that the actor never feels. When Macready played Virginius, after burying his beloved daughter, he confessed that his real experience gave a new force to his acting in the most pathetic situations of the play. Are we to suppose that this was

THE ART OF ACTING

a delusion, or that the sensibility of the man was a genuine aid to the actor? Bannister said of John Kemble that he was never pathetic because he had no children. Talma says that when deeply moved he found himself making a rapid and fugitive observation on the alternation of his voice, and on a certain spasmodic vibration which it contracted in tears. Has not the actor who can thus make his feelings a part of his art an advantage over the actor who never feels, but who makes his observations solely from the feelings of others? It is necessary to this art that the mind should have, as it were, a double consciousness, in which all the emotions proper to the occasion may have full swing, while the actor is all the time on the alert for every detail of his method. It may be that his playing will be more spirited one night than another. But the actor who combines the electric force of a strong

THE ART OF ACTING

personality with a mastery of the resources of his art must have a greater power over his audiences than the passionless actor who gives a most artistic simulation of the emotions he never experiences.

Now, in the practice of acting, a most important point is the study of elocution; and in elocution one great difficulty is the use of sufficient force to be generally heard without being unnaturally loud, and without acquiring a stilted delivery. The advice of the old actors was that you should always pitch your voice so as to be heard by the back row of the gallery—no easy task to accomplish without offending the ears of the front of the orchestra. And I should tell you that this exaggeration applies to everything on the stage. To appear to be natural, you must in reality be much broader than nature. To act on the stage as one really would in a room, would be ineffective and colorless. I never knew an actor who brought the art of elocution to greater perfection than the late Charles Mathews, whose utterance on the stage appeared so natural that one was surprised to find when near him that he was really speaking in a very loud key. There is a great actor in your own country to whose elocution one always listens with the utmost enjoyment—I mean Edwin Booth. He has inherited this gift, I believe, from his famous father, of whom I have heard it said, that he always insisted on a thorough use of the "instruments"—by which he meant the teeth—in the formation of words.

An imperfect elocution is apt to degenerate into a monotonous uniformity of tone. Some wholesome advice on this point we find in the *Life of Betterton.*

"This stiff uniformity of voice is not only displeasing to the ear, but disappoints the effect of the discourse on the hearers; first, by an equal way of speaking, when the pronunciation has everywhere, in every word and every syllable, the same sound, it must inevitably render all parts of speech equal, and so put them on a very unjust level. So that the power of the reasoning part, the lustre and ornament of the figures, the heart, warmth, and vigor of the passionate part being expressed all in the same tone, is flat and insipid, and lost in a supine, or at least unmusical pronunciation. So that, in short, that which ought to strike and stir up the affections, because it is spoken all alike, without any distinction or variety, moves them not at all."

Now, on the question of pronunciation there is something to be said, which, I think, in ordinary teaching is not sufficiently considered. Pronunciation on the stage should be simple and unaffected, but not always fashioned rigidly according to a dictionary standard. No

THE ART OF ACTING

less an authority than Cicero points out that pronunciation must vary widely according to the emotions to be expressed; that it may be broken or cut, with a varying or direct sound, and that it serves for the actor the purpose of color to the painter, from which to draw his variations. Take the simplest illustration, the formal pronunciation of "A-h" is "Ah," of "O-h" "Oh;" but you cannot stereotype the expression of emotion like this. These exclamations are words of one syllable, but the speaker who is sounding the gamut of human feeling will not be restricted in his pronunciation by the dictionary rule. It is said of Edmund Kean that he never spoke such ejaculations, but always sighed or groaned them. Fancy an actor saying thus, "My Desdemona! Oh, ŏh, ŏh!" Words are intended to express feelings and ideas, not to bind them in rigid fetters. The accents of pleasure are different from the

THE ART OF ACTING

accents of pain, and if a feeling is more accurately expressed, as in nature, by a variation of sound not provided for by the laws of pronunciation, then such imperfect laws must be disregarded and nature vindicated. The word should be the echo of the sense.

The force of an actor depends, of course, upon his physique; and it is necessary, therefore, that a good deal of attention should be given to bodily training. Everything that develops suppleness, elasticity, and grace—that most subtle charm—should be carefully cultivated, and in this regard your admirable gymnasium is worth volumes of advice. Sometimes there is a tendency to train the body at the expense of the mind, and the young actor with striking physical advantages must beware of regarding this fortunate endowment as his entire stock-in-trade. That way folly lies, and the result may be too dearly purchased

THE ART OF ACTING

by the fame of a photographer's window. It is clear that the physique of actors must vary; there can be no military standard of proportions on the stage. Some great actors have had to struggle against physical disabilities of a serious nature. Betterton had an unprepossessing face; so had Le Kain. John Kemble was troubled with a weak, asthmatic voice, and yet by his dignity, and the force of his personality, he was able to achieve the greatest effects. In some cases a super-abundant physique has incapacitated actors from playing many parts. The combination in one frame of all the gifts of mind and all the advantages in person is very rare on the stage; but talent will conquer many natural defects when it is sustained by energy and perseverance.

With regard to gesture, Shakespeare's advice is all-embracing. "Suit the action to the word, the word to the action, with

THE ART OF ACTING

this special observance that you over-step not the modesty of nature." And here comes the consideration of a very material part of the actor's business—by-play. This is of the very essence of true art. It is more than anything else significant of the extent to which the actor has identified himself with the character he represents. Recall the scenes between Iago and Othello, and consider how the whole interest of the situation depends on the skill with which the gradual effect of the poisonous suspicion instilled into the Moor's mind is depicted in look and tone, slight of themselves, but all contributing to the intensity of the situation. One of the greatest tests of an actor is his capacity for listening. By-play must be unobtrusive; the student should remember that the most minute expression attracts attention: that nothing is lost, that by-play is as mischievous when it is injudicious as it is effective when rightly con-

THE ART OF ACTING

ceived, and that while trifles make perfection, perfection is no trifle. This lesson was enjoined on me when I was a very young man by that remarkable actress, Charlotte Cushman. I remember that when she played Meg Merrilies I was cast for Henry Bertram, on the principle, seemingly, that an actor with no singing voice is admirably fitted for a singing part. It was my duty to give Meg Merrilies a piece of money, and I did it after the traditional fashion by handing her a large purse full of coin of the realm, in the shape of broken crockery, which was generally used in financial transactions on the stage, because when the virtuous maiden rejected with scorn the advances of the lordly libertine, and threw his pernicious bribe upon the ground, the clatter of the broken crockery suggested fabulous wealth. But after the play Miss Cushman, in the course of some kindly advice, said to me: "Instead of giving me that purse don't you think it would have been much more natural if you had taken a number of coins from your pocket, and given me the smallest? That is the way one gives alms to a beggar, and it would have added to the realism of the scene." I have never forgotten that lesson, for simple as it was, it contained many elements of dramatic truth. It is most important that an actor should learn that he is a figure in a picture, and that the least exaggeration destroys the harmony of the composition. All the members of the company should work towards a common end, with the nicest subordination of their individuality to the general purpose. Without this method a play when acted is at best a disjointed and incoherent piece of work, instead of being a harmonious whole like the fine performance of an orchestral symphony.

The root of the matter is that the actor must before all things form a definite con-

THE ART OF ACTING

ception of what he wishes to convey. It is better to be wrong and be consistent, than to be right, yet hesitating and uncertain. This is why great actors are sometimes very bad or very good. They will do the wrong thing with a courage and thoroughness which makes the error all the more striking; although when they are right they may often be supērb. It is necessary that the actor should learn to think before he speaks; a practice which, I believe, is very useful off the stage. Let him remember, first, that every sentence expresses a new thought and, therefore, frequently demands a change of intonation; secondly, that the thought precedes the word. Of course there are passages in which thought and language are borne along by the streams of emotion and completely intermingled. But more often it will be found that the most natural, the most seemingly accidental effects are obtained when the working of the mind is seen before the tongue gives it words.

You will see that the limits of an actor's studies are very wide. To master the technicalities of his craft, to familiarize his mind with the structure, rhythm, and the soul of poetry, to be constantly cultivating his perceptions of life around him and of all the arts—painting, music, sculpture—for the actor who is devoted to his profession is susceptible to every harmony of color, sound, and form—to do this is to labor in a large field of industry. But all your training, bodily and mental, is subservient to the two great principles in tragedy and comedy—passion and geniality. Geniality in comedy is one of the rarest gifts. Think of the rich unction of Falstaff, the mercurial fancy of Mercutio, the witty vivacity and manly humor of Benedick—think of the qualities, natural and acquired, that are needed for the complete portrayal of such

THE ART OF ACTING

characters, and you will understand how difficult it is for a comedian to rise to such a sphere. In tragedy, passion or intensity sweeps all before it, and when I say passion, I mean the passion of pathos as well as wrath or revenge. These are the supreme elements of the actor's art, which cannot be taught by any system, however just, and to which all education is but tributary.

Now all that can be said of the necessity of a close regard for nature in acting applies with equal or greater force to the presentation of plays. You want, above all things, to have a truthful picture which shall appeal to the eye without distracting the imagination from the purpose of the drama. It is a mistake to suppose that this enterprise is comparatively new to the stage. Since Shakespeare's time there has been a steady progress in this direction. Even in the poet's day every conceivable property was forced into requisition, and his own sense of shortcomings in this respect is shown in *Henry V.* when he exclaims :—

> " Where—O for pity !—we shall much disgrace
> With four or five most vile and ragged foils
> The name of Agincourt."

There have always been critics who regarded care and elaboration in the mounting of plays as destructive of the real spirit of the actor's art. Betterton had to meet this reproach when he introduced scenery in lieu of linsey-woolsey curtains ; but he replied, sensibly enough, that his scenery was better than the tapestry with hideous figures worked upon it which had so long distracted the senses of play-goers. He might have asked his critics whether they wished to see Ophelia played by a boy of sixteen, as in the time of Shakespeare, instead of a beautiful and gifted woman. Garrick did his utmost to improve the mechanical arts of the stage

THE ART OF ACTING

—so much so, indeed, that he paid his scene-painter, Loutherbourg, £500 a year, a pretty considerable sum in those days —though in Garrick's time the importance of realism in costume was not sufficiently appreciated to prevent him from playing Macbeth in a bagwig. To-day we are employing all our resources to heighten the picturesque effects of the drama, and we are still told that this is a gross error. It may be admitted that nothing is more objectionable than certain kinds of realism, which are simply vulgar; but harmony of color and grace of outline have a legitimate sphere in the theatre, and the method which uses them as adjuncts may claim to be "as wholesome as sweet, and by very much more handsome than fine." For the abuse of scenic decoration, the overloading of the stage with ornament, the subordination of the play to a pageant, I have nothing to say. That is all foreign to the artistic purpose

THE ART OF ACTING

which should dominate dramatic work. Nor do I think that servility to archæology on the stage is an unmixed good. Correctness of costume is admirable and necessary up to a certain point, but when it ceases to be "as wholesome as sweet," it should, I think, be sacrificed. You perceive that the nicest discretion is needed in the use of the materials which are nowadays at the disposal of the manager. Music, painting, architecture, the endless variations of costume, have all to be employed with a strict regard to the production of an artistic whole, in which no element shall be unduly obtrusive. We are open to microscopic criticism at every point. When *Much Ado about Nothing* was produced at the Lyceum, I received a letter complaining of the gross violation of accuracy in a scene which was called a cedar-walk. "Cedars!" said my correspondent,—"why, cedars were not introduced into Messina for fifty years after the date of Shakespeare's story!" Well, this was a tremendous indictment, but unfortunately the cedar-walk had been painted. Absolute realism on the stage is not always desirable, any more than the photographic reproduction of Nature can claim to rank with the highest art.

IV.

THE REWARDS OF THE ART.

To what position in the world of intelligence does the actor's art entitle him, and what is his contribution to the general sum of instruction? We are often told that the art is ephemeral; that it creates nothing; that when the actor's personality is withdrawn from the public eye he leaves no trace behind. Granted that his art creates nothing; but does it not often restore? It is true that he leaves nothing like the canvas of the painter and the marble of the sculptor, but has he done nought to increase the general stock of ideas? The astronomer and naturalist create nothing, but they contribute much to the enlightenment of the world. I am taking the highest standard of my art, for I main-

THE ART OF ACTING

tain that in judging any calling you should consider its noblest and not its most ignoble products. All the work that is done on the stage cannot stand upon the same level, any more than all the work that is done in literature. You do not demand that your poets and novelists shall all be of the same calibre. An immense amount of good writing does no more than increase the gayety of mankind; but when Johnson said that the gayety of nations was eclipsed by the death of Garrick, he did not mean that a mere barren amusement had lost one of its professors. When Sir Joshua Reynolds painted Mrs. Siddons as the Tragic Muse, and said he had achieved immortality by putting his name on the hem of her garment, he meant something more than a pretty compliment, for her name can never die. To give genuine and wholesome entertainment is a very large function of the stage, and

THE ART OF ACTING

without that entertainment very many lives would lose a stimulus of the highest value. If recreation of every legitimate kind is invaluable to the worker, especially so is the recreation of the drama, which brightens his faculties, enlarges his vision of the picturesque, and by taking him for a time out of this work-a-day world, braces his sensibilities for the labors of life. The art which does this may surely claim to exercise more than a fleeting influence upon the world's intelligence. But in its highest developments it does more; it acts as a constant medium for the diffusion of great ideas, and by throwing new lights upon the best dramatic literature, it largely helps the growth of education. It is not too much to say that the interpreters of Shakespeare on the stage have had much to do with the widespread appreciation of his works. Some of the most thoughtful students of the poet have recognized their indebtedness to actors, while for multitudes the stage has performed the office of discovery. Thousands who flock to-day to see a representation of Shakespeare, which is the product of much reverent study of the poet, are not content to regard it as a mere scenic exhibition. Without it Shakespeare might have been for many of them a sealed book; but many more have been impelled by the vivid realism of the stage to renew studies which other occupations or lack of leisure have arrested. Am I presumptuous, then, in asserting that the stage is not only an instrument of amusement, but a very active agent in the spread of knowledge and taste? Some forms of stage work, you may say, are not particularly elevating. True; and there are countless fictions coming daily from the hands of printer and publisher which nobody is the better for reading. You cannot have

THE ART OF ACTING

a fixed standard of value in my art; and though there are masses of people who will prefer an unintelligent exhibition to a really artistic production, that is no reason for decrying the theatre, in which all the arts blend with the knowledge of history, manners, and customs of all people, and scenes of all climes, to afford a varied entertainment to the most exacting intellect. I have no sympathy with people who are constantly anxious to define the actor's position, for, as a rule, they are not animated by a desire to promote his interests. "'Tis in ourselves that we are thus and thus;" and whatever actors deserve, socially or artistically, they are sure to receive as their right. I found the other day in a well-circulated little volume a suggestion that the actor was a degraded being because he has a closely-shaven face. This is, indeed, humiliating, and I wonder how it strikes the Roman Catholic

THE ART OF ACTING

clergy. However, there are actors who do not shave closely, and though, alas! I am not one of them, I wish them joy of the spiritual grace which I cannot claim.

It is admittedly unfortunate for the stage that it has a certain equivocal element, which, in the eyes of some judges, is sufficient for its condemnation. The art is open to all, and it has to bear the sins of many. You may open your newspaper, and see a paragraph headed "Assault by an Actress." Some poor creature is dignified by that title who has not the slightest claim to it. You look into a shop-window and see photographs of certain people who are indiscriminately described as actors and actresses though their business has no pretence to be art of any kind.

I was told in Baltimore of a man in that city who was so diverted by the performance of Tyrone Powar, the popular Irish comedian, that he laughed uproariously till the audience was convulsed with merriment at the spectacle. As soon as he could speak, he called out, "Do be quiet, Mr. Showman; do'ee hold your tongue, or I shall die of laughter!" This idea that the actor is a showman still lingers; but no one with any real appreciation of the best elements of the drama applies this vulgar standard to a great body of artists. The fierce light of publicity that beats upon us makes us liable, from time to time, to dissertations upon our public and private lives, our manners, our morals, and our money. Our whims and caprices are discanted on with apparent earnestness of truth, and seeming sincerity of conviction. There is always some lively controversy concerning the influence of the stage. The battle between old methods and new in art is waged everywhere. If an actor were to take to heart everything that is written

THE ART OF ACTING

and said about him, his life would be an intolerable burden. And one piece of advice I should give to young actors is this: Do not be too sensitive; receive praise or censure with modesty and patience. Good honest criticism is, of course, most advantageous to an actor; but he should save himself from the indiscriminate reading of a multitude of comments, which may only confuse instead of stimulating. And here let me say to young actors in all earnestness: Beware of the loungers of our calling, the camp followers who hang on the skirts of the army, and who inveigle the young into habits that degrade their character, and paralyze their ambition. Let your ambition be ever precious to you, and, next to your good name, the jewel of your souls. I care nothing for the actor who is not always anxious to rise to the highest position in his particular walk; but this ideal cannot be cherished by the young man who is induced to fritter away his time and his mind in thoughtless company.

But in the midst of all this turmoil about the stage, one fact stands out clearly : the dramatic art is steadily growing in credit with the educated classes. It is drawing more recruits from those classes. The enthusiasm for our calling has never reached a higher pitch. There is quite an extraordinary number of ladies who want to become actresses, and the cardinal difficulty in the way is not the social deterioration which some people think they would incur, but simply their inability to act. Men of education who become actors do not find that their education is useless. If they have the necessary aptitude—the inborn instinct for the stage—all their mental training will be of great value to them. It is true that there must always be grades in the theatre, that an educated man who is an

THE ART OF ACTING

indifferent actor can never expect to reach the front rank. If he do no more than figure in the army at Bosworth Field, or look imposing in a doorway; if he never play any but the smallest parts; if in these respects he be no better than men who could not pass an examination in any branch of knowledge—he has no more reason to complain than the highly-educated man who longs to write poetry, and possesses every qualification—save the poetic faculty. There are people who seem to think that only irresistible genius justifies any one in adopting the stage as a vocation. They make it an argument against the profession that many enter it from a low sphere of life, without any particular fitness for acting, but simply to earn a livelihood by doing the subordinate and mechanical work which is necessary in every theatre. And so men and women of refinement—especially women—are warned that they

THE ART OF ACTING

must do themselves injury by passing through the rank and file during their term of probation in the actors' craft. Now, I need not remind you that on the stage everybody cannot be great, any more than students of music can all become great musicians; but very many will do sound artistic work which is of great value. As for any question of conduct, Heaven forbid that I should be dogmatic; but it does not seem to me logical that while genius is its own law in the pursuit of a noble art, all inferior merit or ambition is to be deterred from the same path by appalling pictures of its temptations.

If our art is worth anything at all, it is worth the honest, conscientious self-devotion of men and women who, while they may not achieve fame, may have the satisfaction of being workers in a calling which does credit to many degrees of talent. We do not claim to be any better

THE ART OF ACTING

than our fellows in other walks of life. We do not ask the jester in journalism whether his quips and epigrams are always dictated by the loftiest morality; nor do we insist on knowing that the odor of sanctity surrounds the private lives of lawyers and military men before we send our sons into law and the army. It is impossible to point out any vocation which is not attended by temptations that prove fatal to many; but you have simply to consider whether a profession has in itself any title to honor, and then —if you are confident of your capacity— to enter it with a resolve to do all that energy and perseverance can accomplish. The immortal part of the stage is its nobler part. Ignoble accidents and interludes come and go, but this lasts on forever. It lives, like the human soul, in the body of humanity—associated with much that is inferior, and hampered by many hindrances; but it never sinks into nothingness, and never fails to find new and noble work in creations of permanent and memorable excellence. And I would say, as a last word, to the young men in this assembly who may at any time resolve to enter the dramatic profession, that they ought always to fix their minds upon the highest examples; that in studying acting they should beware of prejudiced comparisons between this method and that, but learn as much as possible from all; that they should remember that art is as varied as nature, and as little suited to the shackles of a school; and, above all, that they should never forget that excellence in any art is attained only by arduous labor, unswerving purpose, and unfailing discipline. This discipline is, perhaps, the most difficult of all tests, for it involves the subordination of the actor's personality in every work which is designed to be a complete and harmonious picture. Dramatic art nowadays

THE ART OF ACTING

is more coherent, systematic, and comprehensive than it has sometimes been. And to the student who proposes to fill the place in this system to which his individuality and experience entitle him, and to do his duty faithfully and well, ever striving after greater excellence, and never yielding to the indolence that is often born of popularity—to him I say, with every confidence, that he will choose a career in which, if it does not lead him to fame, he will be sustained by the honorable exercise of some of the best faculties of the human mind.

And now I can only thank you for the patience with which you have listened while, in a slight and imperfect way, I have dwelt with some of the most important of the actor's responsibilities. I have been an actor for nearly thirty years, and what I have told you is the fruit of my experience, and of an earnest and conscientious belief that the calling to which I am proud to belong is worthy of the sympathy and support of all intelligent people.

ADDRESS

AT THE UNIVERSITY OF

OXFORD

26 JUNE

1886

ADDRESS AT THE UNIVERSITY OF OXFORD.

WHEN I was honored by the request of your distinguished Vice-Chancellor to deliver an address before the members of this great University, I told him I could only say something about my own calling, for that I knew little or nothing about anything else. I trust, however, that this confession of the limitations of my knowledge will not prejudice me in your eyes, members as you are—privileged members I may say—of this seat of learning. In an age when so many persons think they know everything, it may afford a not unpleasing variety to meet with some who know that they know nothing.

I cannot discourse to you, even if you wished me to do so, of the respective merits of Æschylus, Sophocles, and Euripides; for if I did, I should not be able to tell you anything that you do not know already. I have not had the advantage —one that very few of the members of my profession in past, or even in present times have enjoyed—of an University education. The only *Alma Mater* I ever knew was the hard stage of a country theatre.

In the course of my training, long before I had taken, what I may call, my degree in London, I came to act in your city. I have a very pleasant recollection of the time I passed here, though I am sorry to say that, owing to the regulation which forbade theatrical performances during term time, I saw Oxford only in vacation, which is rather like—to use the old illustration—seeing *Hamlet* with the part of Hamlet left out. There was then no other building available for dramatic representations than the Town Hall. I may, perhaps, be allowed to congratulate you on the excellent theatre which you now possess—I do not mean the Sheldonian—and at the same time to express a hope that, as a more liberal, and might I say a wiser, *régime* allows the members of the University to go to the play, they will not receive any greater moral injury, or be distracted any more from their studies, than when they were only allowed the occasional relaxation of hearing comic songs. Macready once said that "a theatre ought to be a place of recreation for the sober-minded and intelligent." I trust that, under whatsoever management the theatre in Oxford may be, it will always deserve this character.

You must not expect any learned disquisition from me; nor even in the modi-

FOUR GREAT ACTORS

fied sense in which the word is used among you will I venture to style what I am going to say to you a lecture. You may, by the way, have seen a report that I was cast for *four* lectures; but I assure you there was no ground for such an alarming rumor; a rumor quite as alarming to me as it could have been to you. What I do propose is, to say to you something about four of our greatest actors in the past, each of whom may be termed the representative of an important period in the Annals of our National Drama. In turning over the leaves of a history of the life of Edmund Kean, I came across the following sentence (the writer is speaking of Edmund Kean as having restored Nature to the stage): "There seems always to have been this alternation between the Schools of Nature and Art (if we may so term them) in the annals of the English Theatre." Now if for *Art* I may be allowed to

FOUR GREAT ACTORS

substitute *Artificiality*, which is what the author really meant, I think that his sentence is an epitome of the history of our stage; and it struck me at once that I could not select anything more appropriate—I will not say as a text, for that sounds as if I were going to deliver a sermon—but as the *motif*, or theme of the remarks I am about to address to you. The four actors of whom I shall attempt to tell you something—Burbage, Betterton, Garrick, and Kean—were the *four* greatest champions, in their respective times, on the stage of Nature in contradistinction to Artificiality.

When we consider the original of the Drama, or perhaps I should say of the higher class of Drama, we see that the style of acting must necessarily have been artificial rather than natural. Take the Greek Tragedy, for instance: the actors, as you know, wore masks, and had to speak, or rather intone, in a theatre more than half open to the air, and therefore it was impossible they could employ facial expression, or much variety of intonation. We have not time now to trace at length the many vicissitudes in the career of the Drama, but I may say that Shakespeare was the first dramatist who dared to rob Tragedy of her stilts; and who successfully introduced an element of comedy which was not dragged in by the neck and heels, but which naturally evolved itself from the treatment of the tragic story, and did not violate the consistency of any character.

It was not only with regard to the *writing* of his plays that Shakespeare sought to fight the battle of Nature against Artificiality. However naturally he might write, the affected or monotonous *delivery* of his verse by the actors would neutralize all his efforts. The old rhyming ten-syllable lines could not but lead to a monotonous style of elocution, nor was the early blank verse much improvement in this respect; but Shakespeare fitted his blank verse to the natural expression of his ideas, and not his ideas to the trammels of blank verse.

In order to carry out these reforms, in order to dethrone Artifice and Affectation, he needed the help of actors in whom he could trust, and especially of a leading actor who could interpret his greatest dramatic creations ; such a one he found in Richard Burbage.

Shakespeare came to London first in 1585. Whether on this, his first visit, he became connected with the theatres is uncertain. At any rate it is most probable that he saw Burbage in some of his favorite characters, and perhaps made his acquaintance ; being first employed as a kind of servant in the theatre, and afterwards as a player of inferior parts. It was not until about 1591–1592, that Shakespeare began to turn his attention seriously to dramatic authorship. For five years of his life we are absolutely without any evidence as to what were his pursuits. But there can be little doubt that during this interval he was virtually undergoing a special form of education, consisting rather of the study of human nature than that of books, and was acquiring the art of dramatic construction—learnt better in a theatre than anywhere else. Unfortunately, we have no record of the intercourse between Shakespeare and Burbage; but there can be little doubt that between the dramatist, who was himself an actor, and the actor, who gave life to the greatest creations of his imagination, and who, probably, amazed no less than delighted the great master by the vividness and power of his impersonations, there must have existed a close friendship. Shakespeare, unlike most men of genius, was no bad man of business; and, indeed, a friend of mine, who prides

FOUR GREAT ACTORS

himself upon being a practical man, once suggested that he selected the part of the Ghost in *Hamlet* because it enabled him to go in front of the house between the acts and count the money. Burbage was universally acknowledged as the greatest tragic actor of his time. In Bartholomew Fair, Ben Jonson uses Burbage's name as a synonym for " the best actor"; and Bishop Corbet, in his *Iter Boreale*, tells us that his host at Leicester—

"when he would have said King Richard died,
And call'd, ' A horse ! A horse !' he, Burbage, cried,"

In a scene, in which Burbage and the comedian Kemp (the J. L. Toole of the Shakespearean period) are introduced in *The Return from Parnassus*—a satirical play, as you may know, written by some of the Members of St. John's College, Cambridge, for performance by themselves on New Year's Day, 1602—we have proof of the high estimation in which the great tragic actor was held. Kemp says to the scholars who are anxious to try their fortunes on the stage: "But be merry, my lads, you have happened upon the most excellent vocation in the world for money; they come north and south to bring it to our playhouse; and for honors, who of more report than *Dick Burbage* and *Will Kempe;* he is not counted a gentleman that knows not *Dick Burbage* and *Will Kempe;* there's not a country wench that can dance ' Sellenger's Round,' but can talke of *Dick Burbage* and *Will Kempe.*"

That Burbage's fame as an actor outlived his life may be seen from the description given by Flecknoe:—

"He was a delightful Proteus, so wholly transforming himself into his part, and putting off himself with his clothes, as he never (not so much as in the 'tiring house) assumed himself again until the play was done. . . . He had all the parts of an ex-

FOUR GREAT ACTORS

cellent orator, animating his words with speaking, and speech with acting, his auditors being never more delighted than when he spake, nor more sorry than when he held his peace. Yet even then he was an excellent actor still, never failing in his part when he had done speaking, but with his looks and gestures maintaining it still to the height."

It is not my intention, even if time permitted, to go much into the private life of the four actors of whom I propose to speak. Very little is known of Burbage's private life, except that he was married; perhaps Shakespeare and he may have been drawn nearer together by the tie of a common sorrow; for, as the poet lost his beloved son Hamlet when quite a child, so did Burbage lose his eldest son Richard. Burbage died on March 13th, 1617, being then about 50 years of age: Camden, in his *Annals of James I.*, records his death, and calls him

FOUR GREAT ACTORS

a second Roscius. He was sincerely mourned by all those who loved the dramatic art; and he numbered among his friends Shakespeare, Ben Jonson, Beaumont, and Fletcher, and other "common players," whose names were destined to become the most honored in the annals of English literature. Burbage was the first great actor that England ever saw, the original representative of many of Shakespeare's noblest creations, among others, of Shylock, Richard, Romeo, Hamlet, Lear, Othello, and Macbeth. We may fairly conclude Burbage's acting to have had all the best characteristics of Natural, as opposed to Artificial acting. The principles of the former are so clearly laid down by Shakespeare, in Hamlet's advice to the players, that, perhaps, I cannot do better than to repeat them:—

Speak the speech, I pray you, as I pronounced it to you, trippingly on the tongue: but if you mouth it, as many of your players do, I had as lief the

FOUR GREAT ACTORS

town-crier spoke my lines. Nor do not saw the air too much with your hand, thus, but use all gently; for in the very torrent, tempest, and, as I may say, the whirlwind of passion, you must acquire and beget a temperance that may give it smoothness. O, it offends me to the soul to hear a robustious periwig-pated fellow tear a passion to tatters, to very rags, to split the ears of the groundlings, who for the most part are capable of nothing but inexplicable dumb-show and noise: I would have such a fellow whipped for o'erdoing Termagant; it out-herods Herod; pray you, avoid it. Be not too tame neither, but let your own discretion be your tutor; suit the action to the word, the word to the action; with this special observance, that you o'erstep not the modesty of nature: for anything so overdone is from the purpose of playing, whose end, both at the first and now, was and is, to hold, as 'twere, the mirror up to nature; to show virtue her own feature, scorn her own image, and the very age and body of the time his form and pressure. Now this overdone, or come tardy off, though it make the unskilful laugh, cannot but make the judicious grieve; the censure of the which one must in your allowance o'erweigh a whole theatre of others. O, there be players that I have seen play, and heard others praise, and that highly, not to speak it profanely, that, neither having the accent of Christians

FOUR GREAT ACTORS

nor the gait of Christian, pagan, nor man, have so strutted and bellowed that I have thought some of Nature's journeymen had made men and not made them well, they imitated humanity so abominably.

When we try to picture what the theatre in Shakespeare's time was like, it strikes us that it must have been difficult to carry out those principles. One would think it must have been almost impossible for the actors to keep up the illusion of the play, surrounded as they were by such distracting elements. Figure to yourselves a crowd of fops, chattering like a flock of daws, carrying their stools in their hands, and settling around, and sometimes upon the stage itself, with as much noise as possible. To vindicate their importance in their own eyes they kept up a constant jangling of petty, carping criticism on the actors and the play. In the intervals of repose which they allowed their tongues, they ogled the ladies in the boxes, and made a point

FOUR GREAT ACTORS

of vindicating the dignity of their intellects by being always most inattentive during the most pathetic portions of the play. In front of the house matters were little better: the orange girls going to and fro among the audience, interchanging jokes—not of the most delicate character—with the young sparks and apprentices, the latter cracking nuts or howling down some unfortunate actor who had offended their worships; sometimes pipes of tobacco were being smoked. Picture all this confusion, and add the fact that the female characters of the play were represented by shrill-voiced lads or half-shaven men. Imagine an actor having to invest such representatives with all the girlish passion of a Juliet, the womanly tenderness of a Desdemona, or the pitiable anguish of a distraught Ophelia, and you cannot but realize how difficult under such circumstances *great* acting must have been. In fact, while we are awe-struck by the wonderful intellectuality of the best dramas of the Elizabethan period, we cannot help feeling that certain subtleties of acting, elaborate by-play, for instance, and the finer lights and shades of intonation, must have been impossible. Recitation rather than impersonation would be generally aimed at by the actors.

Thomas Betterton was the son of one of the cooks of King Charles I. He was born in Tothill Street, Westminster, about 1635, eighteen years after the death of Burbage. He seems to have received a fair education; indeed, but for the disturbing effect of the Civil War, he would probably have been brought up to one of the liberal professions. He was, however, apprenticed to a bookseller, who, fortunately for Betterton, took to theatrical management. Betterton was about twenty-four years old when he began his dramatic career.

FOUR GREAT ACTORS

For upwards of fifty years he seems to have held his position as the foremost actor of the day. It was fortunate, indeed, for the interests of the Drama that so great an actor arose at the very time when dramatic art had, as it were, to be resuscitated. Directly the Puritans (who hated the stage and every one connected with it as heartily as they hated their Cavalier neighbors) came into power, they abolished the theatres, as they did every other form of intellectual amusement; and for many years the Drama only existed in the form of a few vulgar "Drolls." It must have been, indeed, a dismal time for the people of England; with all the horrors of civil war fresh in their memory, the more than paternal government allowed its subjects no other amusement than that of consigning their neighbors to eternal damnation, and of selecting for themselves—by anticipation—all the best reserved seats in heaven.

FOUR GREAT ACTORS

When the Restoration took place, the inevitable reaction followed: society, having been condemned to a lengthened period of an involuntary piety—which sat anything but easily on it—rushed into the other extreme; all who wanted to be in the fashion professed but little morality, and it is to be feared that, for once in a way, their practice did not come short of their profession. Now was the time when, instead of "poor players," "fine gentlemen" condescended to write for the stage; and it may be remarked that as long as the literary interests of the theatre were in their keeping, the tone of the plays represented was more corrupt than it ever was at any other period of the history of the Drama. It is something to be thankful for, that at such a time, when the highly-flavored comedies of Wycherley and Congreve were all the vogue, and when the monotonous profligacy of nearly all the characters introduced into those plays was calculated to encourage the most artificial style of acting—it was something, I say, to be thankful for, that at such a time, Betterton, and one or two other actors, could infuse life into the noblest creations of Shakespeare. Owing, more especially, to Betterton's great powers, the tragedy of *Hamlet* held its own in popularity, even against such witty productions as *Love for Love*. It was also fortunate that the same actor who could draw tears as Hamlet, was equally at home in the feigned madness of that amusing rake Valentine, or in the somewhat coarse humor of Sir John Brute. By charming the public in what were the popular novelties of the day, he was able to command their support when he sought it for a nobler form of Drama. He married an actress, Mrs. Saunderson, who was only inferior in her art to her husband. Their married life seems to have been one of perfect happiness. When one hears so much of the profligacy of actors and actresses, and that they are all such a very wicked lot, it is pleasant to think of this couple, in an age proverbial for its immorality, in a city where the highest in rank set an example of shameless licence, living their quiet, pure, artistic life, respected and beloved by all that knew them.

Betterton had few physical advantages. If we are to believe Antony Aston, one of his contemporaries, he had "a short, thick neck, stooped in the shoulders, and had fat, short arms, which he rarely lifted higher than his stomach. His left hand frequently lodged in his breast, between his coat and waistcoat, while with his right hand he prepared his speech." Yet the same critic is obliged to confess that, at seventy years of age, a younger man might have *personated* but could not have *acted*, Hamlet better.

He calls his voice "low and grumbling," but confesses that he had such power over it that he could enforce attention even from fops and orange-girls. I dare say you all know how Steele and Addison admired his acting, and how enthusiastically they spoke of it in *The Tatler*. The latter writes eloquently of the wonderful agony of jealousy and the tenderness of love which he showed in *Othello*, and of the immense effect he produced in *Hamlet*.

Betterton, like all really great men, was a hard worker. Pepys says of him, "Betterton is a very sober, serious man, and studious, and humble, following of his studies ; and is rich already with what he gets and saves." Alas ! the fortune so hardly earned was lost in an unlucky moment: he entrusted it to a friend to invest in a commercial venture in the East Indies which failed most signally. Betterton never reproached his friend, he never murmured at his ill-luck. The friend's daughter was left unprovided for; but Betterton adopted the child, educated her for the stage, and she became an actress of merit, and married Bowman, the player, afterwards known as "The Father of the Stage."

In Betterton's day there were no long runs of pieces; but, had his lot been cast in these times, he might have been compelled to perform, say, *Hamlet* for three hundred or four hundred nights: for the rights of the majority are entitled to respect in other affairs besides politics, and if the theatre-going public demand a play (and our largest theatres only hold a limited number) the manager dare not cause annoyance and disappointment by withdrawing it.

Like Edmund Kean, Betterton may be said to have died upon the stage; for in April, 1710, when he took his last benefit, as Melantius, in Beaumont and Fletcher's *Maid's Tragedy* (an adaption of which, by the way, was played by Macready under the title of *The Bridal*,) he was suffering tortures from gout, and had almost to be carried to his dressing-room; and though he acted the part with all his old fire, speaking these very appropriate words :—

"My heart
And limbs are still the same, my will as great,
To do you service,"

within forty-eight hours he was dead. He was buried in the Cloisters of Westminster Abbey with every mark of respect and honor.

I may here add that the censure said to have been directed against Betterton for the introduction of scenery is the prototype of that cry, which we hear so often nowadays, against over-elaboration in the arrangements of the stage. If it be a crime against good taste to endeavor to enlist every art in the service of the stage, and to heighten the effect of noble poetry by surrounding it with the most beautiful and appropriate accessories, I myself must plead guilty to that charge; but I should like to point out that every dramatist who has ever lived, from Shakespeare downwards, has always endeavored to get his plays put upon the stage with as good effect and as handsome appointments as possible.

Indeed, the Globe Theatre was burned down during the first performance of *King Henry VIII.*, through the firing off of a cannon which announced the arrival of King Henry. Perhaps, indeed, some might regard this as a judgment against the manager for such an attempt at realism.

It was seriously suggested to me by an enthusiast the other day, that costumes of his own time should be used

FOUR GREAT ACTORS

for all Shakespeare's plays. I reflected a little on the suggestion, and then I put it to him whether the characters in *Julius Cæsar* or in *Antony and Cleopatra* dressed in doublet and hose would not look rather out of place. He answered, "He had never thought of that." In fact, difficulties almost innumerable must invariably crop up if we attempt to represent plays without appropriate costume and scenery, the aim of which is to realize the *locale* of the action. Some people may hold that paying attention to such matters necessitates inattention to the acting; but the majority think it does not, and I believe that they are right. What would Alma-Tadema say, for instance, if it were proposed to him that in a picture of the Roman Amphitheatre the figures should be painted in the costume of Spain? I do not think he would see the point of such a noble disregard of detail; and why should he, unless what is false in art is held to be higher than what is true?

Little more than thirty years were to elapse between the death of the honored Betterton and the appearance of David Garrick, who was to restore Nature once more to the stage. In this comparatively short interval progress in dramatic affairs had been all backward. Shakespeare's advice to the actors had been neglected; earnest passion, affecting pathos, ever-varying gestures, telling intonation of voice, and, above all, that complete identification of themselves in the part they represented—all these qualities, which had distinguished the acting of Betterton, had given way to noisy rant, formal and affected attitudes, and a heavy stilted style of declamation. Betterton died in 1710, and six years after, in 1716, Garrick was born. About twenty years after, in 1737, Samuel Johnson and his friend and pupil, David Garrick, set out from Lichfield on their way to London. In spite of the differences in their ages, and their relationship of master and pupil, a hearty friendship had sprung up between them, and one destined, in spite of Johnson's occasional resentment at the actor's success in life, to last till it was ended by the grave. Much of Johnson's occasional harshness and almost contemptuous attitude towards Garrick was, I fear, the result of the consciousness that his old pupil had thoroughly succeeded in life, and had reached the highest goal possible in the career which he had chosen ; while he himself, though looked up to as the greatest scholar of his time, was conscious, as he shows us in his own diary, of how much more he might have done but for his constitutional indolence.

Garrick's family was of French origin, his father having come over to England during the persecution of the Huguenots in 1687, and on his mother's side he had Irish blood in his veins; so that by descent he was a combination of French, English, and Irish, a combination by no means unpromising for one who was going to be an actor.

On reaching London, Garrick enrolled his name in Lincoln's Inn, and was looking about him to see what would turn up, when the news of his father's death reached him. There is no doubt that, if Garrick had consulted his own wishes only, he would at once have gone upon the stage. But fortunately, perhaps, for his future career, he could not bear to grieve his mother's heart by adopting at once, and at such a time when she was crushed with some sorrow for her great loss, a calling which he knew she detested so heartily.

Within a year Mrs. Garrick followed to the grave the husband whom she never ceased to mourn, and David had nothing more to face than the prejudice of his brother, Peter, and of his sisters, if he should resolve ultimately to adopt the profession on which his heart was fixed.

It was not, however, till nearly three years after, in 1741, that Garrick, determined to take the decisive step, first feeling his way by playing Chamont in *The Orphan*, and Sir Harry Wildair, at Ipswich, where he appeared under the name of Mr. Lydall; and under this same name, in the same year, he made his first appearance at Goodman's Fields Theatre, in the part of Richard III. His success was marvellous. Considering the small experience he had had, no actor ever made such a successful *début*. No doubt by waiting and exercising his powers of observation, and by studying many parts in private, he had to a certain extent, matured his powers. But making allowance for all his great natural gifts, there is no denying that Garrick, in one leap, gained a position which, in the case of most other actors, has only been reached through years of toil. He seems to have charmed all classes : the learned and the ignorant, the cultured and the vulgar ; great statesmen, poets, and even the fribbles of fashion were all nearly unanimous in his praise. The dissentient voices were so few that they were drowned in the clamor of applause. Quinn might snarl and growl ; and Horace Walpole, who seems to have grown alarmed at so much of the incense of praise finding its way to the nostrils of another, might give vent to a few feeble sneers ; such as when he said, "I do not mention the things written in his praise because he writes most of them himself." But the battle was won. Nature in the place of Artificiality, Originality in the place of Conventionality, had triumphed on the stage once more.

Consternation reigned in the home at

FOUR GREAT ACTORS

Lichfield when the news arrived that brother David had become a play-actor; but ultimately the family were reconciled to such degradation by the substantial results of the experiment. Such reconcilements are not uncommon. Some young man of good birth and position has taken to the stage; his family, who could not afford to keep him, have been shocked, and in pious horror have cast him out of their respectable circle; but at last success has come, and they have managed to overcome their scruples and prejudices and to profit by the harvest which the actor has reaped.

Garrick seems to have continued playing under the name of Lydall for two months, though the secret must have been an open one. It was not till December the second, the night of his benefit, that he was at last announced under his own name; and henceforward his career was one long triumph, checkered, indeed, by disagreements, quarrels and heart-burnings (for Garrick was extremely sensitive), caused, for the most part, by the envy and jealousy which invariably dog the heels of success.

Second-rate actors, like Theophilus Cibber, or gnats such as Murphy, and others, easily stung him. He was lampooned as "The Sick Monkey" on his return to the stage after having taken a much needed rest. But discretion and audacity seemed to go hand-in-hand, and the self-satisfied satirizer generally over-shoots the mark. Garrick was ever ready with a reply to his assailants; when Dr. Hill attacked his pronunciation, saying that he pronounced his "i's" as if they were "u's," Garrick answered—

"If 'tis true, as you say, that I've injured a letter,
I'll change my note soon, and I hope for the better.
May the just right of letters as well as of men,
Hereafter be fixed by the tongue and the pen.
Most devoutly I wish that they both have their due,
And that *I* may be never mistaken for *U*."

FOUR GREAT ACTORS

Comparing Garrick with Betterton, it must be remembered that he was more exposed to the attacks of envy from the very universality of his success. Never, perhaps, was there a man in any profession who combined so many various qualities. A fair poet, a most fluent correspondent, an admirable conversationalist, possessing a person of singular grace, a voice of marvellous expressiveness, and a disposition so mercurial and vivacious as is rarely found in any Englishman, he was destined to be a great social as well as a great artistic success. He loved the society of men of birth and fashion; he seems to have had a more passionate desire to please in private even than in public, and almost to have justified the often quoted couplet in Goldsmith's "Retaliation."

" On the stage he was natural, simple, affecting,
'Twas only that when he was off he was acting."

Some men, envious of the substantial

fortune which he realized by almost incessant hard work, by thorough good principle with regard to money, and by a noble, not a paltry, economy, might call him mean; though many of them knew well, from their own experience, that his nature was truly generous—his purse, as well as his heart, ever open to a friend, however little he might deserve it. Yet they sneered at his want of reckless extravagance, and called him a miser. The greatest offender in this respect was Samuel Foote, a man of great accomplishments, witty, but always ill-natured. It is difficult to speak of Foote's conduct to Garrick in any moderate language. Mr. Forster may assert that behind Foote's brutal jests there always lurked a kindly feeling; but what can we think of the man who, constantly receiving favors from Garrick's hand, could never speak of him before others without a sneer; who the moment he had received the loan of money or other favor for which he had cringed, snarled—I will not say like a dog, for no dog is so ungrateful—and snapped at the hand which had administered to him of its bounty. When this man, who had never spared a friend, whose whole life had been passed in maligning others, at last was himself a victim of a vile and cruel slander, Garrick forgot the gibes and sneers of which Foote had made him so often the victim, and stood by him with a noble devotion as honorable to himself as it was ill-deserved by its object. Time would not suffice, had I as many hours as I have minutes before me, to tell you of all the acts of generosity that this mean man, this niggardly actor, performed in his lifetime. One characteristic anecdote will suffice. When Whitfield was building his Tabernacle in Tottenham Court Road, he employed one of the carpenters who worked for Garrick at Drury Lane.

FOUR GREAT ACTORS

Subscriptions for the Tabernacle do not seem to have come in as fast as they were required to pay the workmen, so that the carpenter had to go to Garrick to ask for an advance. When pressed for his reason he confessed that he had not received any wages from Mr. Whitfield. Garrick made the advance asked for, and soon after quietly set out to pay a visit to Mr. Whitfield, when, with many apologies for the liberty he was taking, he offered him a five hundred pound bank note as his subscription towards the Tabernacle. Considering that Garrick had no particular sympathy with Nonconformists, this action speaks as much for his charity as a Christian as it does for his liberality as a man.

Perhaps Richard III. remained Garrick's best Shakesperean character. Of course he played Cibber's version and not Shakespeare's. In fact, many of the Shakesperean parts were not played from the poet's own text, but Garrick might have doubted whether even his popularity would have reconciled his audiences to the unadulterated poetry of our greatest dramatist.

Next to Richard, Lear would seem to have been his best Shakesperean performance. In Hamlet and Othello he did not equal Betterton; and in the latter, certainly from all one can discover, he was infinitely surpassed by Edmund Kean. In fact Othello was not one of his great parts. But in the wide range of characters which he undertook, Garrick was probably never equalled. A poor actor named Everard, who was first brought out as a boy by Garrick, says: "Such or such an actor in their respective *fortes* have been allowed to play such or such a part equally well as him; but could they perform Archer and Scrub like him? and Abel Drugger, Ranger, and Bayes, and Benedick; speak his own

FOUR GREAT ACTORS

prologue to *Barbarossa*, in the character of a country-boy, and in a few minutes transform himself in the same play to *Selim ?* Nay, in the same night he has played *Sir John Brute* and the *Guardian*, *Romeo* and *Lord Chalkstone*, *Hamlet* and *Sharp*, *King Lear* and *Fribble*, *King Richard* and the *Schoolboy !* Could anyone but himself attempt such a wonderful variety, such an amazing contrast of character, and be equally great in all? No, no, no! Garrick, take the chair."

Garrick was, without doubt, a very intense actor; he threw himself most thoroughly into any part that he was playing. Certainly we know that he was not wanting in reverence for Shakespeare; in spite of the liberties which he ventured to take with the poet's text, he loved and worshipped him. To Powell, who threatened to be at one time a formidable rival, his advice was, "Never let your Shakespeare be out of your hands; keep him about you as a charm; the more you read him, the more you will like him, and the better you will act." As to his yielding to the popular taste for pantomime and spectacle, he may plead a justification in the words which his friend Johnson put into his mouth in the Prologue that he wrote for the inauguration of his management at Drury Lane :—

> "The Drama's laws the Drama's patrons give,
> And we, who live to please, must please to live."

We must remember how much he did for the stage. Though his alterations of Shakespeare shock us, they are nothing to those outrages committed by others, who deformed the poet beyond recognition. Garrick made Shakespeare's plays once more popular. He purged the actors, for a time at least, of faults that were fatal to any high class of drama, and, above all, he gradually got rid of those abominable nuisances (to which we have already alluded), the people who came and took their seats at the wings, on the stage itself, while the performance was going on, hampering the efforts of the actors and actresses. The stage would have had much to thank Garrick for if he had done nothing more than this—if only that he was the first manager who kept the audience where they ought to be, on the other side of the footlights.

In his private life Garrick was most happy. He was fortunate enough to find for his wife a simple-minded, loyal woman, in a quarter which some people would deem very unpromising. Mrs. Garrick was, as is well-known, a celebrated *danseuse*, known as Mademoiselle Violette, whose real name was Eva Maria Weigel, a Viennese. A more affectionate couple were never seen; they were not blessed with children, but they lived together in the most uninterrupted happiness, and their house was the scene of many social gatherings of a delightful kind. Mrs. Garrick survived her celebrated husband, and lived to the ripe age of ninety-eight, retaining to the very last much of that grace and charm of expression which had won the actor's heart.

Time will not allow me to dwell on the many points of interest in Garrick's career; all of which are to be found in Mr. Percy Fitzgerald's *Life of Garrick*. On returning to London after a visit to the Spensers at Althorp in January, 1779, he was struck down by a fatal attack of his old malady, the gout, and died at the age of sixty-three.

He was buried in Westminster Abbey with ceremonies as imposing as ever graced the funeral of a great man. The pall-bearers were headed by the Duke of Devonshire and the Earl Spenser, while round the grave there were gathered such men as Burke and Fox, and last, not least, his old friend and tutor, Samuel

Johnson, his rugged countenance streaming with tears, his noble heart filled with the sincerest grief. The words so often quoted, artificial though they may seem, came from that heart when, speaking of his dear Davy's death, he said that it " had eclipsed the gayety of nations."

Garrick's remarkable success in society, which achieved for him a position only inferior to that he achieved on the stage, is the best answer to what is often talked about the degrading nature of the actor's profession. Since the days of Roscius no contempt for actors in general, or for their art, has prevented a great actor from attaining that position which is accorded to all distinguished in what are held to be the higher arts.

Nearly nine years after the death of Garrick, on November 4th, 1787, a young woman, who had run away from home when little more than a child to join a company of strolling players, and who,

FOUR GREAT ACTORS

when that occupation failed, earned a scanty living as a hawker in the streets of London, gave birth, in a wretched room near Gray's Inn, to an illegitimate child. This woman was Nancy Carey, the grand-daughter of Henry Carey, the author of the "National Anthem." She was the great-grand-daughter of George Saville, Marquis of Halifax, whose natural son Henry Carey was. A compassionate actress, Miss Tidswell, who knew the father of the child, Aaron Kean, gave her what assistance she could. Poor Nance was removed to her father's lodgings, near Gray's Inn, and there, on the day before mentioned, Edmund Kean was born.

Three months after his birth his mother deserted him, leaving him, without a word of apology or regret, to the care of the woman who had befriended her in her trouble. When he was but three years old he was brought, amongst a number of other children, to Michael Kelly who was then bringing out the opera of *Cymon* at the Opera House in the Haymarket, and, thanks to his personal beauty, he was selected for the part of Cupid. Shortly afterwards he found his way to Drury Lane, where the handsome baby—for he was little more—figured among the imps in the pantomime. Taught here the tricks of the acrobat, he had at four years old acquired such powers of contortion that he was fit to rank as an infant phenomenon. But the usual result followed: the little limbs became deformed, and had to be put in irons, by means of which they regained that symmetry with which nature had at first endowed them. Three years afterwards, in March, 1794, John Kemble was acting Macbeth at Drury Lane; and, in the "cauldron scene," he engaged some children to personate the supernatural beings summoned by the witches from that weird vessel. Little

Edmund with his irons was the cause of a ridiculous accident, and the attempt to embody the ghostly forms was abruptly abandoned. But the child seems to have been pardoned for his blunder, and for a short time was permitted by the manager to appear in one or two children's parts. Little did the dignified manager imagine that the child—who was one of his cauldron of imps in *Macbeth*—was to become, twenty years later, his formidable rival—formidable enough to oust almost the representative of the Classical school from the supremacy he had hitherto enjoyed on the Tragic stage. In Orange Court, Leicester Square, where Holcroft, the author of *The Road to Ruin*, was born, Edmund Kean received his first education. Scanty enough it was, for it had scarcely begun before his wretched mother stepped in and claimed him; and, after her re-appearance, his education seems to have been of a most spasmodic character. Hitherto, the child's experience of life had been hard enough. When only eight years of age he ran away to Portsmouth, and shipped himself on board a ship bound to Madeira. But he found his new life harder than that from which he had escaped, and, by dint of feigning deafness and lameness, he succeeded in procuring his removal to an hospital at Madeira, whence, the doctors finding his case yielded to no remedies, the authorities kindly shipped him again to England. He insisted on being deaf and lame; indeed, so deaf that in a violent thunder-storm he remained perfectly unmoved, explaining his composure by declaring that he could not hear any noise at all. From Portsmouth he made his way on foot to London. On presenting himself at the wretched lodgings where his mother lived, he found that she had gone away with Richardson's troupe. Penniless and half-starving, he suddenly thought of his uncle, Moses Kean, who lived in Lisle Street, Leicester Square, a queer character, who gained a precarious living by giving entertainments as a mimic and ventriloquist. The uncle received his nephew warmly enough, and seems to have cultivated, to the best of his ability, the talent for acting which he recognized at once in the boy. Edmund again enjoyed a kind of desultory education, partly carried on at school and partly at his uncle's home, where he enjoyed the advantage of the kind instructions of his old friend, Miss Tidswell, of D'Egville, the dancing master, of Angelo, the fencing master, and of no less a person than Incledon, the celebrated singer, who seems to have taken the greatest interest in him. But the vagrant, half-gypsy disposition, which he inherited from his mother, could never be subdued, and he was constantly disappearing from his uncle's house for weeks together, which he would pass in going about from one roadside inn to another, amusing the guests with his acrobatic tricks, and his monkey-like imitations. In vain was he locked up in rooms, the height of which from the ground was such as seemed to render escape impossible. He contrived to get out somehow or other, even at the risk of his neck, and to make his escape to some fair, where he would earn a few pence by the exhibition of his varied accomplishments. During these periods of vagabondism he would live on a mere nothing, sleeping in barns, or in the open air, and would faithfully bring back his gains to Uncle Moses. But even this astounding generosity, appealing, as it must have done, to the uncle's sentiments, could not appease him. His uncle went so far, apparently with the concurrence of Miss Tidswell, as to place round the boy's neck a brass collar with the inscription, "This boy belongs to No. 9 Lisle Street; please bring him home." His wandering propensities being for a time subdued, we find the little Edmund again engaged at Drury Lane, and delighting the actors in the greenroom by giving recitations from *Richard III.*, probably in imitation of Cooke; and, on one occasion, among his audience was Mrs. Charles Kemble. During this engagement he played Arthur to Kemble's King John and Mrs. Siddon's Constance, and appears to have made a great success. Soon after this, his uncle Moses died suddenly, and young Kean was left to the severe but kindly guardianship of Miss Tidswell. We cannot follow him through all the vicissitudes of his early career. The sketch I have given of his early life—ample details of which may be found in Mrs. Hawkins's *Life of Edmund Kean*—will give you a sufficient idea of what he must have endured and suffered.

FOUR GREAT ACTORS

When, years afterwards, the passionate love of Shakespeare, which, without exaggeration, we may say he showed almost from his cradle, had reaped its own reward in the wonderful success which he achieved, if we find him then averse to respectable conventionality, erratic, and even dissipated in his habits, let us mercifully remember the bitter and degrading suffering which he passed through in his childhood, and not judge too harshly the great actor. Unlike those whose lives we have hitherto considered, he knew none of the softening influences of a home; to him the very name of mother, instead of recalling every tender and affectionate feeling, was but the symbol of a vague horror, the fountain of that degradation and depravation of his nature, from which no subsequent prosperity could ever redeem it.

For many years after his boyhood his life was one of continual hardship.

FOUR GREAT ACTORS

With that unsubdued conviction of his own powers, which often is the sole consolation of genius, he toiled on and bravely struggled through the sordid miseries of a strolling player's life. The road to success lies through many a thorny course, across many a dreary stretch of desert land, over many an obstacle, from which the fainting heart is often tempted to turn back. But hope, and the sense of power within, which no discouragements can subdue, inspire the struggling artist still to continue the conflict, till at last courage and perseverance meet with their just reward, and success comes. The only feeling then to which the triumphant artist may be tempted is one of good-natured contempt for those who are so ready to applaud those merits which, in the past, they were too blind to recognize. Edmund Kean was twenty-seven years old before his day of triumph came.

FOUR GREAT ACTORS

Without any preliminary puffs, without any flourish of trumpets, on the evening of the 26th January, 1814, soaked through with the rain, Edmund Kean slunk more than walked in at the stage-door of Drury Lane Theatre, uncheered by one word of encouragement, and quite unnoticed. He found his way to the wretched dressing-room he shared in common with three or four other actors; as quick as possible he exchanged his dripping clothes for the dress of Shylock; and, to the horror of his companions, took from his bundle a *black* wig—the proof of his daring rebellion against the great law of conventionality, which had always condemned Shylock to red hair. Cheered by the kindness of Bannister and Oxberry, the latter of whom offered him a welcome glass of brandy and water, he descended to the stage dressed, and peeped through the curtain to see a more than half-empty house. Dr. Drury was waiting at the wings to give him a hearty welcome. The boxes were empty, and there were about five hundred people in the pit, and a few others "thinly scattered to make up a show." Shylock was the part he was playing, and he no sooner stepped upon the stage than the interest of the audience was excited. Nothing he did or spoke in the part was done or spoken in a conventional manner. The simple words, "I will be assured I may," were given with such effect that the audience burst into applause. When the act-drop fell, after the speech of Shylock to Antonio, his success was assured, and his fellow-actors, who had avoided him, now seemed disposed to congratulate him ; but he shrank from their approaches. The great scene with Tubal was a revelation of such originality and of such terrible force as had not probably been seen upon those boards before. "How the devil so few of them could kick up such a row was something marvellous!" naïvely remarked Oxberry. At the end of the third act every one was ready to pay court to him; but again he held aloof. All his thoughts were concentrated on the great "trial" scene, which was coming. In that scene the wonderful variety of his acting completed his triumph. Trembling with excitement, he resumed his half-dried clothes, and, glad to escape, rushed home. He was in too great a state of ecstasy at first to speak, but his face told his wife that he had realized his dream—that he had appeared on the stage of Drury Lane, and that his great powers had been instantly acknowledged. With not a shadow of doubt as to his future, he exclaimed, "Mary, you shall ride in your carriage;" and taking his baby boy from the cradle and kissing him, said, "and Charley, my boy, you shall go to Eton," —and he did.

FOUR GREAT ACTORS

The time when Edmund Kean made his first appearance in London was certainly favorable for an actor of genius. For a long while the national theatre had been in a bad way; and nothing but failure had hitherto met the efforts of the Committee of Management, a committee which numbered among its members Lord Byron. When the other members of the committee, with a strange blindness to their own interests, proposed that for the present, Kean's name should be removed from the bills, Byron interested himself on his behalf: "You have a great genius among you," he said, "and you do not know it." On Kean's second appearance the house was nearly doubled. Hazlitt's criticism had roused the whole body of critics, and they were all there to sit in judgment upon the newcomer. His utter indifference to the audience won him their respect, and before the piece was half over the sentence of the formidable tribunal was in his favor. From that moment Kean exercised over his audiences a fascination which was probably never exercised by any other actor. Garrick was no doubt his superior in parts of high comedy; he was more polished, more vivacious—his manner more distinguished, and his versatility more striking. In such parts as Coriolanus or Rolla, John Kemble excelled him: but in Shylock, in Richard, in Iago, and, above all, in Othello, it may be doubted whether Edmund Kean ever had an equal. As far as one can judge—not having seen Kean one's-self—from the many criticisms extant, written by the most intellectual men, and from the accounts of those who saw him in his prime, he was, to my mind—be it said without any disparagement to other great actors—the greatest genius that our stage has ever seen. Unequal he may have been, perhaps often so, but there were

FOUR GREAT ACTORS

moments in his acting which were, without exaggeration, moments of inspiration. Coleridge is reported to have said that to see Kean act was "like reading Shakespeare by flashes of lightning." This often-quoted sentence embodies perhaps the main feature of Edmund Kean's greatness as an actor; for, when he was impersonating the heroes of our poet, he revealed their natures by an instant flash of light so searching that every minute feature, which by the ordinary light of day was hardly visible, stood bright and clear before you. The effect of such acting was indeed that of lightning—it appalled; the timid hid their eyes, and fashionable society shrank from such heart-piercing revelations of human passion. Persons who had schooled themselves to control their emotion till they had scarcely any emotion left to control, were repelled rather than attracted by Kean's relentless anatomy of all the strongest feeling of our nature. In Sir Giles Overreach, a character almost devoid of poetry, Kean's acting displayed with such powerful and relentless truth the depths of a cruel, avaricious man, baffled in all his vilest schemes, that the effect he produced was absolutely awful. As no bird but the eagle can look without blinking on the sun, so none but those who in the sacred privacy of their imaginations had stood face to face with the mightiest storms of human passion could understand such a performance. Byron, who had been almost forced into a quarrel with Kean by the actor's disregard of the ordinary courtesies of society, could not restrain himself, but rushed behind the scenes and grasped the hand of the man to whom he felt that he owed a wonderful revelation.

I might discant for hours with an enthusiasm which, perhaps, only an actor could feel on the marvellous details of

FOUR GREAT ACTORS

Kean's impersonations. He was not a scholar in the ordinary sense of the word, though Heaven knows he had been schooled by adversity, but I doubt if there ever was an actor who so thought out his part, who so closely studied with the inward eye of the artist the waves of emotion that might have agitated the minds of the beings whom he represented. One hears of him during those early years of struggle and privation, pacing silently along the road, foot-sore and half-starved, but unconscious of his own sufferings, because he was immersed in the study of those great creations of Shakespeare's genius which he was destined to endow with life upon the stage. When you read of Edmund Kean as, alas! he was later on in life, with mental and physical powers impaired, think of the description those gave of him who knew him best in his earlier years; how amidst all the wildness and half-savage Bohemianism, which the miseries of his life had ensured, he displayed, time after time, the most large-hearted generosity, the tenderest kindness of which human nature is capable. Think of him working with a concentrated energy for the one object which he sought, namely, to reach the highest distinction in his calling. Think of him as sparing no mental or physical labor to attain this end, an end which seemed ever fading further and further from his grasp. Think of the disappointments, the cruel mockeries of hope which, day after day, he had to encounter; and then be harsh if you can to those moral failings for which his misfortunes rather than his faults were responsible. If you are inclined to be severe, you may console yourselves with the reflection that this genius, who had given the highest intellectual pleasure to hundreds and thousands of human beings, was hounded by hypocritical sanctimoniousness out of his native land; and though, two years afterwards, one is glad to say, for the honor of one's country, a complete reaction took place, and his reappearance was greeted with every mark of hearty welcome, the blow had been struck from which neither his mind or his body ever recovered. He lingered upon the stage, and died at the age of forty-six, after five years of suffering—almost a beggar—with only a solitary ten-pound note remaining of the large fortune his genius had realized.

It is said that Kean swept away the Kembles and their Classical school of acting. He did not do that. The memory of Sarah Siddons, tragic queen of the British stage, was never to be effaced, and I would remind you that when Kean was a country actor (assured of his own powers, however unappreciated), resenting with passionate pride the idea of playing second to "the Infant Roscius," who was for a time the craze and idol of the hour, "Never," said he, "never; I will play second to no one but John Kemble!" I am certain that when his better nature had the ascendency no one would have more generously acknowledged the merits of Kemble than Edmund Kean. It is idle to say that because his style was solemn and slow, Kemble was not one of the greatest actors that our stage has produced. It is only those whose natures make them incapable of approbation or condemnation in artistic matters without being partisans, who, because they admire Edmund Kean, would admit no merit in John Kemble. The world of art, thank Heaven, is wide enough for both, and the hearts of those who truly love art are large enough to cherish the memory of both as of men who did noble work in the profession which they adorned. Kean blended the Realistic with the

FOUR GREAT ACTORS

Ideal in acting, and founded a school of which William Charles Macready was, afterwards, in England, the foremost disciple.

Thus have we glanced, briefly enough, at four of our greatest actors whose names are landmarks in the history of the Drama in England, the greatest Drama of the world. We have seen how they all carried out, by different methods perhaps, but in the same spirit, the principle that in acting Nature must dominate Art. But it is Art that must interpret Nature; and to interpret the thoughts and emotions of her mistress should be her first object. But those thoughts, those emotions, must be interpreted with grace, with dignity and with temperance; and these, let us remember, Art alone can teach.

ADDRESS

SESSIONAL OPENING

PHILOSOPHICAL INSTITUTION

EDINBURGH

9 NOVEMBER

1891

THE ART OF ACTING

HAVE chosen as the subject of the address with which I have the honor to inaugurate for the second time the Session of the Edinburgh Philosophical Institution, "The Art of Acting." I have done so, in the first instance, because I take it for granted that when you bestow on any man the honor of asking him to deliver the inaugural address, it is your wish to hear him speak of the subject with which he is best acquainted; and the Art of Acting is the subject to which my life has been devoted. I have another reason also which, though it may, so far as you are concerned, be

THE ART OF ACTING

personal to those of my calling, I think it well to put before you. It is that there may be, from the point of view of an actor distinguished by your favor, some sort of official utterance on the subject. There are some irresponsible writers who have of late tried to excite controversy by assertions, generally false and always misleading, as to the stage and those devoted to the arts connected with it. Some of these writers go so far as to assert that Acting is not an Art at all; and though we must not take such wild assertions quite seriously, I think it well to place on record at least a polite denial of their accuracy. It would not, of course, be seemly to merely take so grave an occasion as the present as an opportunity for such a controversy, but as I am dealing with the subject before you, I think it better to place you in full knowledge of the circumstances. It does not do, of course, to pay too much attention to ephemeral writings, any more than to creatures of the mist and the swamp and the night. But even the buzzing of the midge, though the insect may be harmless compared with its more poison-laden fellows, can divert the mind from more important things. To disregard entirely the world of ephemera, and their several actions and effects were to deny the entirety of the scheme of creation.

I take it for granted that in addressing you on the subject of the Art of Acting I am not, *prima facie*, encountering set prejudices; for had you despised the Art which I represent I should not have had the honor of appearing before you to-day. You will, I trust, on your part, bear this in mind, and I shall, on my part, never forget that you are members of a Philosophical Institution, the very root and basis of whose work is to inquire into the heart of things with the purpose of dis-

THE ART OF ACTING

covering why such as come under your notice are thus or thus.

The subject of my address is a very vast one, and is, I assure you, worthy of a careful study. Writers such as Voltaire, Schlegel, Goethe, Lessing, Charles Lamb, Hazlitt, and Schiller, have not disdained to treat it with that seriousness which Art specially demands—which anything in life requires whose purpose is not immediate and imperative. For my own part I can only bring you the experience of more than thirty years of hard and earnest work. Out of wide experience let me point out that there are many degrees of merit, both of aim, of endeavor, and of execution in acting, as in all things. I want you to think of acting at its best—as it may be, as it can be, as it has been, and is—and as it shall be, whilst it be followed by men and women of strong and earnest purpose. I do not for a moment wish you to be-

THE ART OF ACTING

lieve that only Shakespeare and the great writers are worthy of being played, and that all those efforts that in centuries have gathered themselves round great names are worthy of your praise. In the House of Art are many mansions where men may strive worthily and live cleanly lives. All Art is worthy, and can be seriously considered, so long as the intention be good and the efforts to achieve success be conducted with seemliness. And let me here say, that of all the arts none requires greater intention than the art of acting. Throughout it is necessary to *do* something, and that something cannot fittingly be left to chance, or the unknown inspiration of a moment. I say "unknown," for if known, then the intention is to reproduce, and the success of the effort can be in nowise due to chance. It may be, of course, that in moments of passionate excitement the mind grasps some new

THE ART OF ACTING

idea, or the nervous tension suggests to the mechanical parts of the body some new form of expression; but such are accidents which belong to the great scheme of life, and not to this art, or any art, alone. You all know the story of the painter who, in despair at not being able to carry out the intention of his imagination, dashed his brush at the imperfect canvas, and with the scattering paint produced by chance the very effect which his brush guided by his skill alone, had failed to achieve. The actor's business is primarily to reproduce the ideas of the author's brain, to give them form, and substance, and color, and life, so that those who behold the action of a play may, so far as can be effected, be lured into the fleeting belief that they behold reality. Macready, who was an earnest student, defined the art of the actor "to fathom the depths of character, to trace its latent motives, to feel its

THE ART OF ACTING

finest quivering of emotion, is to comprehend the thoughts that are hidden under words, and thus possess one's-self of the actual mind of the individual man"; and Talma spoke of it as "the union of grandeur without pomp, and nature without triviality"; whilst Shakespeare wrote, "the purpose of playing, whose end, both at the first and now, was and is, to hold, as 'twere, the mirror up to nature ; to show virtue her own feature, scorn her own image, and the very age and body of the time his form and pressure."

This effort to reproduce man in his moods is no mere trick of fancy carried into execution. It is a part of the character of a strong nation, and has a wider bearing on national life than perhaps unthinking people are aware. Mr. Froude, in his survey of early England, gives it a special place; and I venture to quote his words, for they carry with them, not only their own lesson, but the authority of a great name in historical research.

"No genius can dispense with experience; the aberrations of power, unguided or ill-guided, are ever in proportion to its intensity, and life is not long enough to recover from inevitable mistakes. Noble conceptions already existing, and a noble school of execution which will launch mind and hand at once upon their true courses, are indispensable to transcendent excellence; and Shakespeare's plays were as much the offspring of the long generations who had pioneered his road for him, as the discoveries of Newton were the offspring of those of Copernicus.

"No great general ever arose out of a nation of cowards; no great statesman or philosopher out of a nation of fools; no great artist out of a nation of materialists; no great drama, except when the

THE ART OF ACTING

drama was the possession of the people. Acting was the especial amusement of the English, from the palace to the village green. It was the result and expression of their strong, tranquil possession of their lives, of their thorough power over themselves, and power over circumstances. They were troubled with no subjective speculations; no social problems vexed them with which they were unable to deal; and in the exuberance of vigor and spirit, they were able, in the strict and literal sense of the word, to play with the materials of life." So says Mr. Froude.

In the face of this statement of fact set forth gravely in its place in the history of our land, what becomes of such bold assertions as are sometimes made regarding the place of the drama being but a poor one, since the efforts of the actor are but mimetic and ephemeral, that they pass away as a tale that is told? All

THE ART OF ACTING

art is mimetic; and even life itself, the highest and last gift of God to His people, is fleeting. Marble crumbles, and the very names of great cities become buried in the dust of ages. Who then would dare to arrogate to any art an unchanging place in the scheme of the world's development, or would condemn it because its efforts fade and pass? Nay, more; has even the tale that is told no significance in after years? Can such not stir, when it is worth the telling, the hearts of men, to whom it comes as an echo from the past? Have not those tales remained most vital and most widely known which are told and told again and again, face to face and heart to heart, when the teller and the listener are adding, down the ages, strength to the current of a mighty thought or a mighty deed and its record?

Surely the record that lives in the minds of men is still a record, though it

THE ART OF ACTING

be not graven on brass or wrought in marble. And it were a poor conception of the value of any art, if, in considering it, we were to keep our eyes fixed on some dark spot, some imperfection, and shut our eyes to its aim, its power, its beauty. It were a poor age indeed where such a state of things is possible; as poor as that of which Mrs. Browning's unhappy poet spoke in the bitterness of his soul:

> " The age culls simples,
> With a broad clown's back turned broadly to the glory of the stars."

Let us lift our faces when we wish to judge truly of any earnest work of the hand or mind of man, and see it placed in the widest horizon that is given to us. Poetry, painting, sculpture, music, architecture, all have a bearing on their time, and beyond it; and the actor, though his knowledge may be, and must be, limited by the knowledge of his age, so long as he sound the notes of human passion, has something which is common to all the ages. If he can smite water from the rock of one hardened human heart—if he can bring light to the eye or wholesome color to the faded cheek—if he can bring or restore in ever so slight degree the sunshine of hope, of pleasure, of gayety, surely he cannot have worked in vain. It would need but a small effort of imagination to believe that that great wave theory, which the scientists have proved as ruling the manifestations of light and sound, applies also to the efforts of human emotion. And who shall tell us the ultimate bounds of these waves of light and sound? If these discernible waves can be traced till they fade into impalpable nothingness, may we not think that this other, impalpable at the beginning as they are at the end, can alone stretch into the dimness of memory? Sir Joshua's gallant compliment, that he

THE ART OF ACTING

achieved immortality by writing his name on the hem of Mrs. Siddons's garment, when he painted her as the Tragic Muse, had a deeper significance than its pretty fancy would at first imply.

Not for a moment is the position to be accepted that the theatre is merely a place of amusement. That it is primarily a place of amusement, and is regarded as such by its *habitués*, is of course apparent; but this is not its limitation. For authors, managers, and actors it is a serious employment, to be undertaken gravely, and of necessity to be adhered to rigidly. Thus far it may be considered from these different stand-points; but there is a larger view—that of the State. Here we have to consider a custom of natural growth specially suitable to the genius of the nation. It has advanced with the progress of each age, and multiplied with its material prosperity. It is a living power, to be used for good,

THE ART OF ACTING

or possibly for evil ; and far-seeing men recognize in it, based though it be on the relaxation and pleasures of the people, an educational medium of no mean order. Its progress in the past century has been the means of teaching to millions of people a great number of facts which had perhaps otherwise been lost to them. How many are there who have had brought home to them in an understandable manner by stage-plays the costumes, habits, manners, and customs of countries and ages other than their own ; what insight have they thus obtained into facts and vicissitudes of life—of passions and sorrows and ambitions outside the narrow scope of their own lives, and which yet may and do mould the destinies of men. All this is education—education in its widest sense, for it broadens the sympathies and enlarges the intellectual grasp. And beyond this again—for these are advantages on the material side—

THE ART OF ACTING

there is that higher education of the heart, which raises in the scale of creation all who are subject to its sweetening influences. To hold his place therefore amongst these progressing forces, the actor must at the start be well endowed with some special powers, and by training, reading, and culture of many kinds, be equipped for the work before him. No amount of training can give to a dense understanding and a clumsy personality certain powers of quickness and spontaneity; and, on the other hand, no genius can find its fullest expression without some understanding of the principles and method of a craft. It is the actor's part to represent or interpret the ideas and emotions which the poet has created, and to do this he must at the first have a full knowledge and understanding of them. This is in itself no easy task. It requires much study and much labor of many kinds. Having then acquired an idea,

THE ART OF ACTING

his intention to work it out into reality must be put in force ; and here new difficulties crop up at every further step taken in advance. Now and again it suffices the poet to think and write in abstractions ; but the actor's work is absolutely concrete. He is brought in every phase of his work into direct comparison with existing things, and must be judged by the most exacting standards of criticism. Not only must his dress be suitable to the part which he assumes, but his bearing must not be in any way antagonistic to the spirit of the time in which the play is fixed. The free bearing of the sixteenth century is distinct from the artificial one of the seventeenth, the mannered one of the eighteenth, and the careless one of the nineteenth. And all this quite exclusive of the minute qualities and individualities of the character represented. The voice must be modulated to the vogue of the time. The habitual action

THE ART OF ACTING

of a rapier-bearing age is different to that of a mail-clad one—nay, the armor of a period ruled in real life the poise and bearing of the body ; and all this must be reproduced on the stage, unless the intelligence of the audience, be they ever so little skilled in history, is to count as naught.

It cannot therefore be seriously put forward in the face of such manifold requirements that no Art is required for the representation of suitable action. Are we to imagine that inspiration or emotion of any kind is to supply the place of direct knowledge of facts—of skill in the very grammar of craftsmanship? Where a great result is arrived at much effort is required, whether the same be immediate or has been spread over a time of previous preparation. In this nineteenth century the spirit of education stalks abroad and influences men directly and indiréctly, by private generosity and national fore-

THE ART OF ACTING

sight, to accumulate as religiously as in former ages ecclesiastics and devotees gathered sacred relics, all that helps to give the people a full understanding of lives and times and countries other than their own. Can it be that in such an age all that can help to aid the inspiration and to increase direct knowledge is of no account whatever, because, forsooth, it has a medium or method of its own? There are those who say that Shakespeare is better in the closet than on the stage ; that dramatic beauty is more convincing when read in private than when spoken on the stage to the accompaniment of suitable action. And yet, if this be so, it is a strange thing that, with all the activity of the new-born printing-press, Shakespeare's works were not known to the reading public till the fame of the writer had been made on the stage. And it is a stranger thing still, if the drama be a mere poetic form of words, that the

THE ART OF ACTING

writer who began with *Venus and Adonis*, when he found the true method of expression to suit his genius, ended with *Hamlet* and *The Tempest*.

How is it, I ask, if these responsible makers of statements be correct, that every great writer down from the days of Elizabeth, when the drama took practical shape from the wish of the poets to render human life in all its phases, have been desirous of seeing their works, when written in dramatic form, represented on the stage—and not only represented, but represented under the most favorable conditions obtainable, both as to the fitness of setting and the choice of the most skilled and excellent players? Are we to take it that the poet, with his eye in a fine phrenzy rolling, sees all the minute details of form, color, light, sound, and action which have to be rendered complete on the stage? Is there nothing in what the individual actor, who is gifted

THE ART OF ACTING

with fine sense and emotional power, can add to mere words, however grand and rolling in themselves, and whatsoever mighty image they may convey? Can it be possible that there is any sane person who holds that there is no such thing as expression in music so long as the written notes are correctly rendered—that the musical expression of a Paganini or a Liszt, or that the voice of a Malibran or a Grisi, has no special charm—nay more, that there is not some special excellence in the instruments of Amati or Stradivarius? If there be, we can leave to him, whilst the rest of mankind marvel at his self-sufficient obtuseness, to hold that it was nothing but his own imagination which so much influenced Hazlitt when he was touched to the heart by Edmund Kean's rendering of the words of the remorseful Moor, "Fool, fool, fool!" Why, the action of a player who knows how to convey to the audience that he is

THE ART OF ACTING

listening to another speaking, can not only help in the illusion of the general effect, but he himself can suggest a running commentary on what is spoken. In every moment in which he is on the stage, an actor accomplished in his craft can convey ideas to the mind.

It is in the representation of passion that the intention of the actor appears in its greatest force. He wishes to do a particular thing, and so far the wish is father to the thought that the brain begins to work in the required direction, and the emotional faculties and the whole nervous and muscular systems follow suit. A skilled actor can count on this development of power, if it be given to him to rise at all to the height of a passion ; and the inspiration of such moments may, now and again, reveal to him some new force or beauty in the character which he represents. Thus he will gather in time a certain habitual strength in a par-

THE ART OF ACTING

ticular representation of passion. Diderot laid down a theory that an actor never feels the part he is acting. It is of course true that the pain he suffers is not real pain, but I leave it to any one who has ever felt his own heart touched by the woes of another to say if he can even imagine a case where the man who follows in minutest detail the history of an emotion, from its inception onward, is the only one who cannot be stirred by it—more especially when his own individuality must perforce be merged in that of the archetypal sufferer. Talma knew that it was possible for an actor to feel to the full a simulated passion, and yet whilst being swept by it to retain his consciousness of his surroundings and his purpose. In his own words—"The intelligence accumulates and preserves all the creations of sensibility." And this is what Shakespeare means when he makes Hamlet tell the players—"for in the

THE ART OF ACTING

very torrent, tempest, and, as I may say, whirlwind of your passion, you must beget a temperance that may give it smoothness."

How can any one be temperate in the midst of his passion, lest it be that his consciousness and his purpose remain to him? Let me say that it is this very discretion which marks the ultimate boundary of an Art, which stands within the line of demarcation between Art and Nature. In Nature there is no such discretion. Passion rules supreme and alone; discretion ceases, and certain consequences cease to be any deterrent or to convey any warning. It must never be forgotten that all Art has the aim or object of seeming and not of being; and that to understate is as bad as to overstate the modesty or the efflorescence of Nature. It is not possible to show within the scope of any Art the entire complexity and the myriad combining influ-

THE ART OF ACTING

ences of Nature. The artist has to accept the conventional standard—the accepted significance—of many things, and confine himself to the exposition of that which is his immediate purpose. To produce the effect of reality it is necessary, therefore, that the efforts of an artist should be slightly different from the actions of real life. The perspective of the stage is not that of real life, and the result of seeming is achieved by means which, judged by themselves, would seem to be indirect. It is only the raw recruit who tries to hit the bull's-eye by point-blank firing, and who does not allow for elevation and windage. Are we to take it for a moment, that in the Art of Acting, of which elocution is an important part, nothing is to be left to the individual idea of the actor? That he is simply to declaim the words set down for him, without reference to the expression of his face, his bearing, or his action? It is in the union

THE ART OF ACTING

of all the powers—the harmony of gait and utterance and emotion—that conviction lies. Garrick, who was the most natural actor of his time, could not declaim so well as many of his own manifest inferiors in his art—nay, it was by this that he set aside the old false method, and soared to the heights in which, as an artist, he reigned supreme. Garrick personated and Kean personated. The one had all the grace and mastery of the powers of man for the conveyance of ideas, the other had a mighty spirit which could leap out in flame to awe and sweep the souls of those who saw and heard him. And the secret of both was that they best understood the poet—best impersonated the characters which he drew, and the passions which he set forth.

In order to promote and preserve the idea of reality in the minds of the public, it is necessary that the action of the play

THE ART OF ACTING

be set in what the painters call the proper *milieu*, or atmosphere. To this belongs costume, scenery, and all that tends to set forth time and place other than our own. If this idea be not kept in view there must be, or at all events there may be, some disturbing cause to the mind of the onlooker. This is all—literally all—that dramatic Art imperatively demands from the paint room, the wardrobe, and the property shop ; and it is because the public taste and knowledge in such matters have grown that the actor has to play his part with the surroundings and accessories which are sometimes pronounced to be a weight or drag on action. Suitability is demanded in all things ; and it must, for instance, be apparent to all that the things suitable to a palace are different to those usual in a hovel. There is nothing unsuitable in Lear in kingly raiment in the hovel in the storm, because such is here demanded by the exigencies

THE ART OF ACTING

of the play : but if Lear were to be first shown in such guise in such a place with no explanation given of the cause, either the character or the stage-manager would be simply taken for a madman. This idea of suitability should always be borne in mind, for it is in itself a sufficient answer to any thoughtless allegation as to overloading a play with scenery.

Finally, in the consideration of the Art of Acting, it must never be forgotten that its ultimate aim is beauty. Truth itself is only an element of beauty, and to merely reproduce things vile and squalid and mean is a debasement of Art. There is apt to be such a tendency in an age of peace, and men should carefully watch its manifestations. A morose and hopeless dissatisfaction is not a part of a true national life. This is hopeful and earnest, and, if need be, militant. It is a bad sign for any nation to yearn for, or even to tolerate, pessimism in its enjoy-

THE ART OF ACTING

ment; and how can pessimism be other than antagonistic to beauty? Life, with all its pains and sorrows, is a beautiful and a precious gift; and the actor's Art is to reproduce this beautiful thing, giving due emphasis to those royal virtues and those stormy passions which sway the destinies of men. Thus the lesson given by long experience—by the certain punishment of ill-doing—and by the rewards that follow on bravery, forbearance, and self-sacrifice, are on the mimic stage conveyed to men. And thus every actor who is more than a mere machine, and who has an ideal of any kind, has a duty which lies beyond the scope of his personal ambition. His art must be something to hold in reverence if he wishes others to hold it in esteem. There is nothing of chance about this work. All, actors and audience alike, must bear in mind that the whole scheme of the higher Drama is not to be regarded as a game in life which

THE ART OF ACTING

can be played with varying success. Its present intention may be to interest and amuse, but its deeper purpose is earnest, intense, sincere.

THE END.

www.ingramcontent.com/pod-product-compliance
Lightning Source LLC
Chambersburg PA
CBHW032229230426
43666CB00033B/1647